Physical Characteristics of Toy Manchester Terrier

(from the American Kennel Club's breed stan

Body: Overall, slightly longer than tall. The height, measured vertically from the ground to the highest point of the withers, is slightly less than the length, measured horizontally from the point of the shoulders to the rear projection of the upper thigh.

Tail: Moderately short reaching no further than the hock joint. It is set on at the end of the croup. Being thicker where it joins the body, the tail tapers to a point. The tail is carried in a slight upward curve, but never over the back.

Hindquarters: Thigh should be muscular with the length of the upper and lower thighs being approximately equal. The stifle is well turned. The well let down hocks should not turn in nor out as viewed from the rear. The hind legs are carried well back.

Feet: Front feet are compact and well arched. The two middle toes should be slightly longer than the others. The pads should be thick and the toenails should be jet black. The hind feet are shaped like those of a cat with thick pads and jet black nails.

Size: Shall not exceed 12 pounds.

Toy Manchester Terrier

By Peter Brown

9 **History of the** Toy Manchester Terrier

Meet the early terriers of England to see how the Manchester and Toy Manchester Terriers developed. Learn about the breed's ratting heritage, other breeds in its background and the people responsible for the establishment of this delightful small black and tan dog.

21 **Characteristics of the** Toy Manchester Terrier

The best of the terrier traits in an elegant small package, the Toy Manchester Terrier is an agile, skilled, intelligent and personable dog that makes a charming, compact companion. The pros and cons of the breed are discussed, along with breed-specific health concerns of which every prospective owner should be aware.

26 **Breed Standard for the** Toy Manchester Terrier

Learn the requirements of a well-bred Toy Manchester Terrier by studying the descriptions of the breed as set forth by the American Kennel Club. Both show dogs and pets must possess key characteristics as outlined in the standard.

34 **Your Puppy** Toy Manchester Terrier

Be advised about choosing a reputable breeder and selecting a healthy, typical puppy. Understand the responsibilities of ownership, including home preparation, acclimatization, the vet and prevention of common puppy problems.

67 **Everyday Care of Your** Toy Manchester Terrier

Enter into a sensible discussion of dietary and feeding considerations, exercise, grooming, traveling and identification of your dog. This chapter discusses Toy Manchester Terrier care for all stages of development.

84 **Training Your** Toy Manchester Terrier

By Charlotte Schwartz
Be informed about the importance of training your Toy Manchester Terrier from the basics of housebreaking and understanding the development of a young dog to executing obedience commands (sit, stay, down, etc.).

Contents

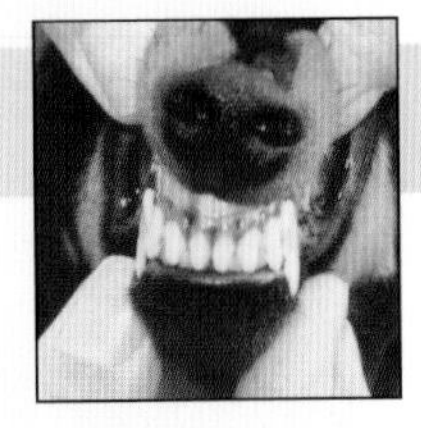

Health Care of Your Toy Manchester Terrier **109**

Discover how to select a qualified vet and care for your dog at all stages of life. Topics include vaccinations, skin problems, dealing with external and internal parasites and common medical and behavioral conditions.

Your Senior Toy Manchester Terrier **140**

Consider the care of your senior Toy Manchester Terrier, including the proper diet for a senior. Recognize the signs of an aging dog, both behavioral and medical; implement a special-care program with your vet and become comfortable with making the final decisions and arrangements for your senior Toy Manchester Terrier.

Showing Your Toy Manchester Terrier **144**

Enter the world of showing dogs. Learn about the American Kennel Club, the different types of shows and the making of a champion. Go beyond the conformation ring to find out about agility, obedience trials and more.

Behavior of Your Toy Manchester Terrier **150**

Learn to recognize and handle behavioral problems that may arise with your Toy Manchester Terrier. Topics discussed include separation anxiety, aggression, barking, chewing, digging, begging, etc.

Index 156

KENNEL CLUB BOOKS: **TOY MANCHESTER TERRIER**

ISBN: 1-59378-351-5

308 Main Street, Allenhurst, NJ 07711 USA

Cover Design Patented: US 6,435,559 B2 • Printed in South Korea

Photos by Carol Ann Johnson with additional photographs by:
Norvia Behling, T. J. Calhoun, Carolina Biological Supply, Doskocil, Isabelle Français, James Hayden-Yoav, James R. Hayden, RBP, Bill Jonas, Dwight R. Kuhn, Dr. Dennis Kunkel, Mikki Pet Products, Phototake, Jean Claude Revy, Alice Roche, Dr. Andrew Spielman and Alice van Kempen.

The owner wishes to thank the owners of the dogs featured in this book, including John Richardson and Alan Taylor.

Illustrations by Patricia Peters.

Originating in its namesake city in England, the Toy Manchester Terrier has been a distinct breed for more than half a century. In its native England, the breed is called the English Toy Terrier.

HISTORY OF THE TOY MANCHESTER TERRIER

As the name suggests, the Manchester Terrier originated in Manchester, England some time back in the early 1500s, although this breed name was not used until the late 19th century. All indications are that the breed evolved from the original Black and Tan Terrier and the Old English Terrier, believed to be the most ancient of the British terriers, having existed in Britain for 400 to 500 years.

In ancient times, these noble black and tan hunters were cherished for their keen sense of smell and hearing. Some accounts describe these original specimens, used mainly as ratters, as very high-strung and a bit snappy. Fortunately, these undesirable characteristics have been selectively bred out over the generations, and the Manchester's alert nature and clown-like charm have remained in today's Toy variety. Feisty terrier-dog qualities certainly added to the Manchester's value as an expert mouse- and rat-killer! The breed's strong desire to chase prey, and its extreme loyalty to man, will undoubtedly remain a part of its character, even if the Toy variety never hunts more than a

The Standard Manchester Terrier is virtually the identical to the Toy variety except in size. A Standard can weigh twice as much as a Toy.

stray mouse or "dust bunny."

Most histories of the breed point to an 18th-century gentleman by the name of John Hulme as the key figure responsible for the breed's development. It was Hulme's breeding experiments with England's common Black and Tan Terrier and the graceful, speedy Whippet that gave rise to the Manchester Terrier we know today. Specific traits certainly point to these crossbreedings. Selective breeding resulted in a speedy and agile little hunter, which quickly went on to become a prized and most sought-after rodent killer. The Manchester's expertise as an excellent little tracking and hunting companion even placed the breed in the saddlebags of hunters that sought fox. There is some speculation (but no specific proof) that some West Highland White Terrier and Doberman Pinscher bloodlines were also introduced into the breed at some later point in time. Even today, the Manchester's color, coat texture and genetic makeup are very similar to that of the Doberman Pinscher. Still others theorize that the Italian Greyhound and Dachshund also played a role in the creation of the Manchester Terrier.

The Manchester itself is credited as the foundation for the development of other breeds, including the popular Doberman Pinscher; the Australian Terrier; the German Hunting Terrier, known in its native land as Deutscher Jagdterrier; the little-known British herding dog, the Lancashire Heeler; and the Moscow Toy Terrier, all of which

TWO VARIETIES OF ONE GREAT DOG

The Manchester Terrier comes in two varieties—Standard and Toy. The Standard variety must weigh in at more than 11 pounds. Some Standards may be slightly heavier than 22 pounds, but this disqualifies them as show dogs. The Toy variety is virtually the same as the Standard, except it must weigh 11 pounds or less. Although registered by the AKC as the same breed, the Toy variety is a member of the Toy Group and the Standard belongs to the Terrier Group.

Sylvia Sidney, a world-famous screen star of yesteryear, was a supporter of the Manchester Terrier breeds. She is shown here with her favorite Standard. Note the cropped ears on this British dog from the 1930s.

are black and tan in color, though varying in size and purpose. Another American breed believed to be related to the Manchester is called the Louisiana Squirrel Dog, an unregistered working dog from the South.

England, of course, is the home of most of the Terrier Group breeds, and the Manchester Terrier reached the United States, Canada and the rest of Europe by the 19th century. They were initially bred to be vermin hunters. They were also loyal lap dogs that excelled at chasing and catching mice and rats in homes and on ships.

Eventually, the breed's talent for killing rats turned into a recreational sport for the English people, a sport very much favored by Mr. Hulme himself. In fact, these little brave dogs were placed in the rat pits, and bets were taken to see which dog could kill the greatest number of rats in a certain time period. Thankfully, this blood sport, along with other kinds of animal baiting and dog fighting, eventually lost support when more civilized minds came to the fore. Nevertheless, despite bad taste and stomach-turning gore, the Manchester was quite adept at speed-killing his ratine foe. The history books state that a 5-pound

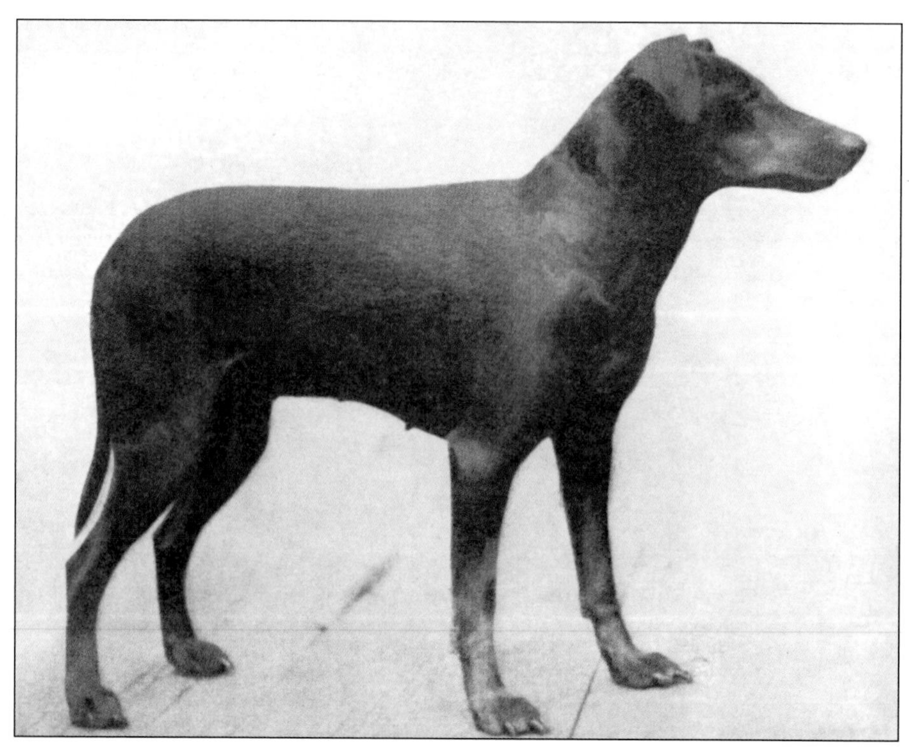

Eng. Ch. Threlkeld Cliff, bred by Miss C. S. Ratcliff in 1927. She became an English Champion in 1932.

Eng. Ch. Prince Rufus, bred by Mr. W. Anstey in 1932, was one year old when he became an English Champion.

Manchester Terrier named "Tiny" reportedly killed 300 rats in 54 minutes and 50 seconds! It was a gory but extraordinary accomplishment for any dog, especially one so small!

Reaching the height of its public appeal in the Victorian era, the breed was admired for its sharp, sleek outline as well as its ability to keep the stables vermin-free and to hunt rabbit and other small game. While men preferred the large Manchesters, it was the refined ladies who became enamored with the smaller dogs, as this was a period of celebrated miniatures, including paintings, sculptures and dogs! As breeders saw the rise in demand for the smaller dogs, they began breeding specifically for the diminutive size. By repeatedly breeding the smallest to the smallest, the Toy variety emerged. Unfortunately, this practice was taken to the extreme, and many tiny but unhealthy toy terriers were produced. Fortunately, today's Toy variety is consistent in type and temperament, and actually much larger and healthier than the specimens that were found in days of Queen Victoria.

EARLY ENGLISH INFLUENCE

The Black and Tan Terrier was one of the breeds mentioned by Dr. Johannes Caius in the famous letter

Banjo came from one of the leading Manchester Terrier kennels at the end of the 19th century. He was owned by S. Dean, and the Dean affix became a hallmark of excellence in the breed.

of 1570 concerning the dogs of England. The work was sent to Gesner for inclusion in his encyclopedic work on the dogs of all nations. It wasn't long before the Manchester district of England became known for two "poor men's sports"—rat killing and rabbit coursing. It was a time of poor sanitation, and rats were running wild. The tremendous rat population was a great menace to health in populated areas, and the country desperately needed relief, which came in the form of an efficient rodent killer. By 1860, the city of Manchester became the breed's center. Their popularity quickly spread over the British Isles before coming to America and expanding

PLACE YOUR BETS

Since ancient times, the Manchester Terrier was cherished for its sharp hunting skills. Using the breed's talented instincts as a vermin killer, the English developed a sport that included wagering on these terriers. A dog was placed in a giant pit and then timed to see how many rats it could dispose of.

FAMOUS OWNERS OF MANCHESTERS

Beloved American President Teddy Roosevelt and famous mystery novelist Agatha Christie both owned Manchesters. President Roosevelt's dog "Blackjack" lived in the White House with him. Christie owned two Manchesters, named "Treacle" and "Bingo," both of whom were inspirations for her novels.

across the rest of Europe. In 1874, The Kennel Club Stud Book was established and the distinctive terrier breed evolved.

Because there were several breeds that were part of the Manchester's development, there really isn't a single dominant individual dog or single foundation strain to which the breed can be traced specifically. The Manchester's popularity in England remained somewhat moderate and the breed was never excessively popular—much to the delight of dedicated breeders and fanciers.

In 1895, at the apex of the Manchester's popularity, ear cropping was outlawed in England and this proved a disastrous blow to the breed's popularity. Up until this time, the Manchester's ears, which

Prince George, a favorite in the 1890s, was typical of the Manchester Terrier breed during those times.

were heavy and pendulous when not cut, had always been cropped to give the breed the desired alert expression. Once ear cropping could not be performed on the dogs' ears, many people disliked the spoiled expression of the natural-eared Manchester Terrier. It took several years of breeding to develop sharp and attractive button ears, which are now desirable in the Standard variety.

The early 1900s brought a resurgence of the breed to England. Over the years there have been many influential English Manchester breeders that have stamped their bloodlines. It's impossible to list them all and their outstanding stock, but one person's breeding in particular does deserve mention. Mrs. Greene's Harford Kennels, which developed in the 1930s, was responsible for two outstanding dogs that later made their way to American soil. They were Golden Embkem of Hartford and Golden Ermine of Harford. The Harford kennel would go on to produce several other influential dogs.

After World War II, there were only 5 breedable Manchesters left in all of England (it is said that there were 11 total, 6 of which were too old or infertile). Dogs sent over from the US revived the breed in England, using matings to the Miniature Black and Tans (the designation of the smaller Manchesters assigned between the World Wars). Beginning in 1960, the smaller dogs then became registered as English Toy Terriers and could not be crossed with Standard Manchesters. It took ten years for the breed to regain its status in the UK, and new champions began emerging around 1955. The British Manchester Terrier Club remained the only parent club to continue on after World War II, and it was the members of this club and their colleagues in the US who are rightly credited for reviving the breed in England.

A MATTER OF BLACK OR WHITE

Black and tan is the only color combination acceptable for the Manchester Terrier. However, this wasn't always the case. In the mid-1800s, there was some interest in different color variations, including white, blue and red. These never gained favor with hunters, who preferred dogs to be black or white, so as not to be mistaken for their fox-red quarry. Eventually the English White Terrier also lost favor, due to significant health problems in the breed.

THE MANCHESTER IN AMERICA

In November 1877, at the Philadelphia Grand National Dog Show, there was the first class for Black and Tan Terriers. All of the dogs that participated that day weighed less than 10 pounds. The

An excellent head and ears of a Standard Manchester Terrier. Attractive button ears are a desirable trait in the Standard variety, but not acceptable in the Toy.

TINY THE WONDER

A Toy Manchester named Tiny the Wonder had the distinction of slaying 300 rats during a pit contest in record time, just under 55 minutes. A historic moment for Manchesters, and a sad one for the rat fancy!

breed was next represented at the Gilmore's Garden Westminster Show in 1878. It wasn't until 1887 that the first Black and Tan was registered. The dog's name was "Lever," and he would later become the first recognized Manchester Terrier. For the next 40 years, the Toy Manchester Terrier was registered in the classification "Toy Terriers other than Yorkshires." The breed was known as the Toy Black and Tan up until 1934 when it officially became the Toy Manchester Terrier. A dog named "Harvester Lassie," owned by H. T. Thompson, was the first true Manchester Terrier registered.

In 1883, Mrs. G. Campbell Schmidt imported the first Black and Tan to America. This was the beginning of the Campbell breeding empire that would continue for many, many years. Campbell kennels were responsible for many leading strains in America. Many of today's winning Manchester bloodlines can still be traced to some of these influential dogs.

In 1923, the Manchester Terrier Club of America was founded and the breed name was officially changed from Toy Black and Tan Terrier to Toy Manchester Terrier. In 1938, the American Toy Manchester Club was accepted by the American Kennel Club. Up until 1959, the Manchester Terrier and the Toy Manchester Terrier were registered as two separate breeds, although interbreeding between the two breeds was permitted. Since then, the breed has been registered as one, with two varieties, the Toy and the Standard. In the UK, The Kennel Club registers the breed as the English Toy Terrier (Black and Tan). The American Manchester Terrier Club was formed in 1958 and remains as the parent club for both varieties of the breed.

Many top American kennels developed before and after World Wars I and II. Mrs. Ruby Owens from Aurora, Illinois was the breeder-owner of one of the finest Standard specimens of the breed. The dog's name was Ch. Kricket of Kent. The dog was one of the first to earn a Best in Show. Ch. White's Black Prince, bred and owned by Dr. Howard S. M. White of Sioux City, Iowa, and Ch. Evan's Clipper, stamped themselves as superb representatives of the breed during this era.

Although the list of influential American Manchester Terrier breeders and dogs is numerous, it would be unfair not to list some of the more noteworthy establishments. Many of the kennels listed have held their own for decades and continue to operate strongly, thus showing no signs of diminishing any time soon. Others are no longer in operation, but will forever be remembered for helping to keep the breed strong. They include Russell (R.D. Clark of Glen Allen, Virginia), Cawdor (G. Calder Little of Fullerton, Maryland), Dempsey (Mrs. Dixie Dempsey of Houston, Texas, Carrman-Kent (Mrs. Ruby Owens of Aurora, Illinois), Kay Ess (Mrs. K.S. Waters of La Porte, Indiana.), Dusky (Mrs. A.H. Reiman of San Francisco, California), and White (Dr. H.S.M. White of Sioux City, Iowa.). Some of the early influential sires and dams included Ch. Dempsey's Tippy Tin, Ch. Russell's Sport of Harford, Ch. Johnny Zero of Kent, Ch. Bell Boy, Ch. White's Black Midas, Ch. Tony's Zkay and Ch. Lady Blondin.

The breed was a relatively popular dog in Canada around 1950, though today the breed has become only rarely seen. The fairly newly formed Canadian Manchester Terrier Club, established in 1998, seeks the recognition of the Canadian Kennel Club and exists to promote the breed's best interest in that country.

The Toy Manchester Terrier enjoys moderate popularity around the world, including the US, where the Toy and Standard varieties are registered as the same breed but are shown in separate classes and Groups.

Meet one of the world's most easy-care dogs: easy to train, easy to groom and easy to transport!

CHARACTERISTICS OF THE TOY MANCHESTER TERRIER

IS THE TOY MANCHESTER RIGHT FOR YOU?

Such a handsome small dog, with a distinctive black and tan coat that sheds only minimally, the Toy Manchester Terrier holds the distinction of being the dog world's best kept secret. While similar—but inferior—breeds have sparked the public's interest and led towards damaging popularity, the Toy Manchester has never been more than the companion of the well-informed dog fancier. Toy Manchester owners are a very selective group of dog lovers, who do not succumb to the estimable charms of breeds like the Toy Fox Terrier, the Miniature Pinscher or, heaven forbid, the Rat Terrier! The Toy Manchester Terrier arguably is the most elegant, sophisticated and gifted Toy dog in the Group!

A TRUE FAMILY COMPANION

The Toy Manchester Terrier is extremely bright and active. His stable temperament and handsome looks have made him a choice companion and alarm dog. For a family that welcomes a small dog, the Toy Manchester makes an excellent companion for almost every household. They are virtually odorless and adapt very well to their environment. However, the breed's intelligence can be very challenging to his new owner. Toy Manchester puppies can be very demanding. They require constant attention and cherish family interaction right through adolescence. They can be

A Toy Manchester Terrier is not for everyone—only the most discerning of dog lovers. This tiny dog is delicate and charming, and makes a bright and active family member.

sensitive and should always be trained using positive reinforcement. If you choose a young puppy, expect him to chew anything that is accessible. Like other breeds, all new puppies should be carefully supervised at all times, and safely crated when left for extended periods.

THINGS TO CONSIDER

The Toy Manchester Terrier has moderate exercise requirements. Daily exercise is not an absolute necessity for the breed, but they do enjoy daily walks or runs and welcome the opportunity to be outdoors. They do equally well in a apartment settings, average-sized houses and large farms. They are not picky eaters and will accept most any diet.

The Toy Manchester is a quick learner. This is the reason why the breed has done very well in all types of performance sport activities, including agility and obedience. They love to please their owners and will go to extremes to do so. They are energetic, affectionate and loving to their families, and thrive on human attention and interaction. They bond very easily. Despite the Toy Manchester's loyalty to his owners and immediate family, he can be reserved with strangers. In fact, he makes a good watchdog and will bark to alert his owner of possible danger. Frequently, the breed's bark is a lot louder than its bite.

The Toy Manchester does very well with children and other pets (even cats, though never small rodent types), provided the pets are properly introduced and socialized. Their dynamic personality will keep children busy for hours while enjoying each other's company.

The breed is very clean and usually easier to house-train than most other toys and terriers. This is rather unusual for a toy breed, as most others can be rather difficult to housebreak. This is not the case with the Manchester. Even small puppies will learn to housebreak in a relatively short time. The key to success is patience and repetition. It won't be long before your Toy Manchester understands what is expected of him.

If you are looking for a dog that requires minimal grooming, you've made an excellent choice. The Toy Manchester requires little in the way of grooming. Their lack of undercoat is a relief for allergy sufferers. Individuals who suffer from allergy-related problems usually find the breed less irritating. Despite the Toy Manchester's short coat, he does shed a little. The only difference is that it's usually more difficult to notice.

Because of the short coat, the Toy Manchester is very sensitive to the cold. If exposed to subfreezing temperatures for long periods of time, the Manchester should be outfitted with a warm coat or sweater (made especially for dogs). Many vendors at dog shows or on websites sell suitable dog clothing. The Toy Manchester Terrier is a hardy little tyke, but cannot stay outdoors when the weather is cold or damp. Like all toy breeds, the Toy Manchester prefers the comfortable amenities of his family's home. Of course, every dog, even those primarily kept indoors, needs ample time to enjoy the fresh air and to have the opportunity to stretch his legs.

The Toy Manchester is a wonderful breed and is sure to give you and your family many years of fun and entertainment. This is a long-lived breed, with Toy Manchesters commonly living to 15 or more years. While the author's loyalty and love of the Toy Manchester is painting a rosy photo of this "near-perfect" canine, it must be confessed that the breed is not for everyone. Although they are extremely loving and loyal to their families, they can be wary of strangers. Not trusting of strangers or other unknowns, the Toy Manchester is a cautious type, unlike the overly demonstrative retrievers and herding dogs. The Toy Manchester is a confident little dog, and does not exhibit fear-biting behavior, which is a problem with some other Napoleon-complex-suffering toy dogs. The breed is neither dog-aggressive nor aggressive with humans, though they prefer the company of friends, people and dogs whom they know and trust.

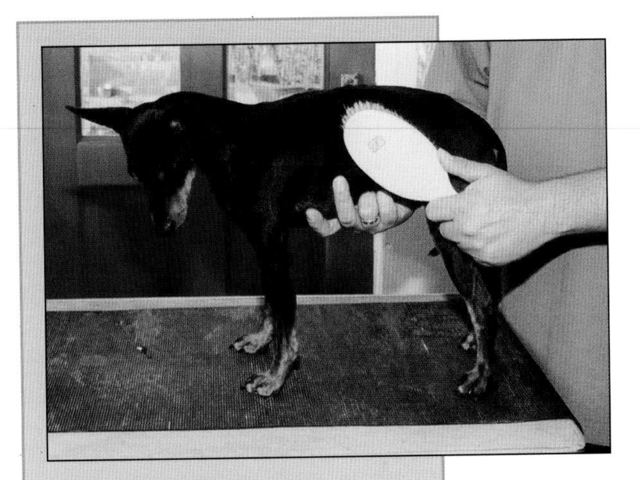

SKIN AND COAT CARE

The Toy Manchester Terriers' short coat makes the breed vulnerable to extreme cold and to injury. Dog bites or roughhousing with other dogs can cause visible scars. These scars usually heal easily, but can be somewhat unsightly. Many Manchester owners, especially those involved in dog shows, intentionally keep the coats shiny by applying extra oils to the dogs' skin and bathing the dog less often.

HEALTH CONCERNS OF THE TOY MANCHESTER

Fortunately for the breed and those who love it, the Toy Manchester is a healthy breed of dog. It's not uncommon for a well-bred, properly cared-for Manchester of either variety to live to 14 to 16 years old or more. The Toy Manchester is a strong, hardy little dog, resistant to many of the common ailments that frequently affect other dogs. Although they are susceptible to a few genetic problems, these conditions are quite rare. Following are some of the more common health concerns that have been known to affect the Manchester varieties. The breed has been associated with von Willebrand's disease, thyroid problems and Leggs-Calves-Perthes. Reputable breeders should be aware of these problems and do their best to remove dogs with their conditions from their breeding programs.

Von Willebrand's Disease

Von Willebrand's disease is a serious bleeding disorder that is common in several breeds, including Manchester Terriers (both Toys and Standards), Doberman Pinschers, Scottish Terriers and Shetland Sheepdogs. Dogs that are affected can bleed to death from minor injuries because their blood does not properly clot as a result of a deficiency of the von Willebrand factor, a plasma protein. Fortunately, the condition can be eliminated through proper selection of sire and dam.

Recently, a genetic test has been developed to help diagnose the disorder. This test can tell you if your dog has been affected, is a carrier of the disease, or is clear of the gene responsible for the disorder.

If you are considering acquiring a Toy Manchester Terrier, you must ask your breeder about von Willebrand's disease in his bloodlines. Reputable breeders that are using the new testing should be able to let you know whether there's any chance of your puppy's having the disorder. Unfortunately, if your dog is affected, there is no cure. Some treatments have been developed to improve clotting time, but their effectiveness still remains uncertain.

Legges-Calves-Perthes

Legges-Calves-Perthes is a condition that results in the degeneration of the femur bone. The ailment is very common in small breeds, and has even been described as the "small dog's hip dysplasia." The condition results

CURBING AT FIRST BARK

Manchesters are excellent watchdogs. However, their bark is usually bigger than their bite, and excessive barking can be a real problem. They have a frequent tendency to bark at everything and everyone! It's highly recommended that a Toy Manchester puppy be exposed to many different surroundings and situations to combat the problem.

in a lack of blood flow to the bone. As a result, the femur does not receive an adequate supply of nourishment, and the bone begins to deteriorate. The condition usually appears in dogs that are six to nine months of age.

The first signs or symptoms of the disease is when a dog favors his rear legs. If your Toy Manchester develops any signs that he might be suffering from discomfort or pain, he should be brought to the veterinarian immediately. An x-ray will determine whether or not the condition is present. Surgery can be performed for dogs that are affected with the disease. If the surgery is successful, dogs can lead relatively normal lives. Affected dogs should not be used in any breeding programs.

Thyroid Problems

Manchester Terriers can also be prone to thyroid problems. The thyroid is an important gland that is responsible for regulating body functions, including weight and hair growth. If you suspect that your Toy Manchester might have a thyroid condition (unusual hair loss or weight gain), a simple blood test can determine if there's a problem. The thyroid can produce too much or too little hormone levels. The condition can usually be corrected with a simple pill provided by your veterinarian.

A PERFECT LAP DOG

The Toy Manchester is a very active dog with a lively nature. They are loyal companion dogs and, because of their size, can be comfortable as lap dogs.

BREED STANDARD FOR THE

TOY MANCHESTER TERRIER

All of the breeds currently recognized by the American Kennel Club (AKC) for registration have a breed standard, which is drafted by the breed's parent club and approved by the AKC. The standard portrays what experts would consider to be the "ideal" representative of the breed. The standard is not the representation of any actual dog, but simply a theory of what such a perfect specimen would look like. Breed standards are used as the guidelines for dog shows worldwide, assisting breeders, judges and exhibitors in envisioning the correct type, structure and balance for a given breed. Most breed standards also list faults and disqualifications, so that which is not desired is also specified.

In a typical dog show, a judge will evaluate every competitor that is shown before him on that given day. The dog that most closely resembles the standard in the judge's determination is the dog that is placed first in his class. All judges have their own interpretations, and not every judge will agree on what dog is best. That's what makes conformation competition an exciting and appealing sport. There is a different judging panel at each show, and therefore different opinion as to which dogs most closely adhere to the standard.

CAN THE STANDARD HELP YOU?

The breed standard can be a very valuable asset for novice and experienced dog owners, dog breeders and show judges alike. Any person interested in buying a puppy or adult Toy Manchester Terrier and who is not conversant with what is correct for this breed should read and study the breed standard. It is a valuable guideline in determining the physical qualities that make up your breed of choice, and any disqualifications of which fanciers should be aware before buying, breeding or judging a dog. Although the "perfect" dog portrayed in the breed standard will likely never exist, it is in the owner's best interest to attempt to obtain a dog that closely resembles it.

If you can learn to understand what your breed should look like and its main function, you can select a dog that's healthy, physically sound and a worthy representative of the breed. Any reputable breeder should understand the breed standard and strive to produce dogs that closely resemble it.

The same AKC standard is used for both varieties of Manchester Terrier, as they are simply different sizes of the same dog. The few slight differences in requirements are detailed in the standard.

AMERICAN KENNEL CLUB STANDARD FOR THE MANCHESTER TERRIER

General Appearance

A small, black, short-coated dog with distinctive rich mahogany markings and a taper style tail. In structure the Manchester presents a sleek, sturdy, yet elegant look, and has a wedge-shaped, long and clean head with a keen, bright, alert expression. The smooth, compact, muscular body expresses great power and agility, enabling the Manchester to kill vermin and course small game.

Except for size and ear options, there are no differences between the Standard and Toy varieties of the Manchester Terrier. The Toy is a diminutive version of the Standard variety.

Size, Proportion, Substance

The *Toy variety* shall not exceed 12 pounds. It is suggested that clubs consider dividing the American-bred and Open classes by weight as follows: 7 pounds and under, over 7 pounds and not exceeding 12 pounds.

The *Standard variety* shall be over 12 pounds and not exceeding 22 pounds. Dogs weighing over 22 pounds shall be disqualified. It is suggested that clubs consider dividing the American-bred and Open classes by weight as follows: over 12 pounds and not exceeding 16

A Toy Manchester Terrier of correct type, balance and structure in profile.

A Toy Manchester Terrier head study, showing correct type.

pounds, over 16 pounds and not exceeding 22 pounds.

The Manchester Terrier, overall, is slightly longer than tall. The height, measured vertically from the ground to the highest point of the withers, is slightly less than the length, measured horizontally from the point of the shoulders to the rear projection of the upper thigh.

The bone and muscle of the Manchester Terrier is of sufficient mass to ensure agility and endurance.

Head

The Manchester Terrier has a keen and alert **expression**.

The nearly black, almond shaped **eyes** are small, bright, and sparkling. They are set moderately close together, slanting upwards on the outside. The eyes neither protrude nor sink in the skull. Pigmentation must be black.

Correct **ears** for the *Standard variety* are either the naturally erect ear, the cropped ear, or the button ear. No preference is given to any of the ear types. The naturally erect ear, and the button ear, should be wider at the base tapering to pointed tips, and carried well up on the skull. Wide, flaring, blunt tipped, or "bell" ears are a serious fault. Cropped ears should be long, pointed and carried erect.

The only correct **ear** for the *Toy variety* is the naturally erect ear. They should be wider at the base tapering to pointed tips, and carried well up on the skull. Wide, flaring, blunt tipped, or "bell" ears are a serious fault. Cropped, or cut ears are a disqualification in the Toy variety.

The **head** is long, narrow, tight skinned, and almost flat with a slight indentation up the forehead. It resembles a blunted wedge in frontal and profile views. There is a visual effect of a slight *stop* as viewed in profile.

The **muzzle** and **skull** are equal in length. The *muzzle* is well filled under the eyes with no visible cheek muscles. The underjaw is full and well defined and the **nose** is black.

Tight black *lips* lie close to the jaw. The jaws should be full and powerful with full and proper **dentition**. The teeth are white and strongly developed with a true scissors bite. Level bite is acceptable.

Neck, Topline, Body

The slightly arched **neck** should be slim and graceful, and of moderate length. It gradually becomes larger as it approaches, and blends smoothly with the sloping shoulders. Throatiness is undesirable.

The **topline** shows a slight arch over the robust loins falling slightly to the tail set. A flat

In addition to correct physical structure and movement, a winning Toy Manchester must exhibit the desirable keen and alert temperament in the ring.

back or roached back is to be severely penalized.

The *chest* is narrow between the legs and deep in the brisket. The forechest is moderately defined. The *ribs* are well sprung, but flattened in the lower end to permit clearance of the forelegs.

The *abdomen* should be tucked up extending in an arched line from the deep brisket.

The taper style **tail** is moderately short reaching no further than the hock joint. It is set on at the end of the croup. Being thicker where it joins the body, the tail tapers to a point. The tail is carried in a slight upward curve, but never over the back.

Forequarters

The *shoulder blades* and the *upper arm* should be relatively the same length. The distance from the elbow to the withers should be approximately the same as the distance from the elbow to the ground. The *elbows* should lie close to the brisket. The *shoulders* are well laid back.

The *forelegs* are straight, of proportionate length, and placed well under the brisket. The pasterns should be almost perpendicular.

The **front feet** are compact and well arched. The two middle toes should be slightly longer than the others. The pads should be thick and the toenails should be jet black.

Hindquarters

The *thigh* should be muscular with the length of the upper and lower thighs being approximately equal. The stifle is well turned.

The well let down hocks should not turn in nor out as viewed from the rear. The hind legs are carried well back.

The **hind feet** are shaped like those of a cat with thick pads and jet black nails.

Coat

The coat should be smooth, short, dense, tight, and glossy; not soft.

COLOR
The coat color should be jet black and rich mahogany tan, which should not run or blend into each other, but abruptly form clear, well defined lines of color. There shall be a very small tan spot over each eye, and a

Body Faults in Profile

Short neck, upright shoulders, weak pasterns, straight in rear.

Upright shoulders, roached back, ring tail, weak rear, cow-hocked, ewe-necked.

Ewe-necked, loaded shoulders, wide front, steep in croup, low tail set and weak rear.

Short-necked, loaded upright shoulders, dip in topline, straight in rear, toes out (east-west) front, tail carriage suggesting shyness, long back.

very small tan spot on each cheek. On the head, the muzzle is tanned to the nose. The nose and nasal bone are jet black. The tan extends under the throat, ending in the shape of the letter V. The inside of the ears are partly tan. There shall be tan spots, called "rosettes," on each side of the chest above the front legs. These are more pronounced in puppies than in adults. There should be a black "thumbprint" patch on the front of each foreleg at the pastern. The remainder of the foreleg shall be tan to the carpus joint. There should be a distinct black "pencil mark" line running lengthwise on the top of each toe on all four feet. Tan on the hind leg should continue from the pencilling on the toes up the inside of the legs to a little below the stifle joint. The outside of the hind legs should be black. There should be tan under the tail, and on the vent, but only of such size as to be covered by the tail.

White on any part of the coat is a serious fault, and shall disqualify whenever the white shall form a patch or stripe measuring as much as one half inch at its longest dimension.

Any color other than black and tan shall be disqualified.

Color and/or markings should never take precedence over soundness and type.

Gait
The gait should be free and effortless with good reach of the forequarters, showing no indication of hackney gait. Rear quarters should have strong, driving power to match the front reach. Hocks should fully extend. Each rear leg should move in line with the foreleg of the same side, neither thrown in nor out. When moving at a trot, the legs tend to converge towards the center of gravity line beneath the dog.

Temperament
The Manchester Terrier is neither aggressive nor shy. He is keenly observant, devoted, but discerning. Not being a sparring breed, the Manchester is generally friendly with other dogs. Excessive shyness or aggressiveness should be considered a serious fault.

Disqualifications
Standard variety—Weight over 22 pounds.
Toy variety—Cropped or cut ears.
Both varieties—White on any part of the coat whenever the white shall form a patch or stripe measuring as much as one half inch at its longest dimension.
Any color other than black and tan.

Approved June 10, 1991
Effective July 31, 1991

The Toy Manchester is examined on the table by the judge, who will go over the dog with a physical hands-on inspection.

TOY MANCHESTER TERRIER

HOW TO SELECT A PUPPY

Before reaching the decision that you will definitely look for a Toy Manchester puppy, it is essential that you are fully clear in your mind that this is absolutely the most suitable breed for you and for your family. There is no disputing the fact that this is a very special breed, and all the pros and cons must be carefully weighed against each other before reaching the important decision that a Toy Manchester is going to become part of your home and your life.

This Boston Terrier has a new family member, a baby Toy Manchester. Properly introduced, these two will become the closest of pack-mates.

"YOU BETTER SHOP AROUND!"

Finding a reputable breeder who sells healthy pups is very important, but make sure that the breeder you choose is not only someone you respect but also someone with whom you feel comfortable. Your breeder will be a resource long after you buy your puppy, and you must be able to call with reasonable questions without being made to feel like a pest! If you don't connect on a personal level, investigate some other breeders before making a final decision.

Once you have made that decision, you must also ask yourself why you want a Toy Manchester, whether purely as a pet or as a show dog. This should be made clear to the breeder when you make your initial inquiries, for you will certainly need to take the breeder's advice as to which available puppy displays the most promise for the show ring.

If looking for a pet, you should discuss your family situation with the breeder, and again take his advice as to which puppy is likely to suit you best.

Watch the puppies interact together, and see which little personality appeals to you most. Obviously you will also take into account the overall quality of the dog, especially if destined for a show home. And never be tempted to take pity on an unduly shy puppy, for in doing so you will be asking for trouble in the long term, as such a dog is likely to encounter problems in socializing.

PUPPY PERSONALITY

When a litter becomes available to you, choosing a pup out of all those adorable faces will not be an easy task! Sound temperament is of utmost importance, but each pup has its own personality and some may be better suited to you than others. A feisty, independent pup will do well in a home with older children and adults, while quiet, shy puppies will thrive in a home with minimal noise and distractions. Your breeder knows the pups best and should be able to guide you in the right direction.

Visiting a litter is as educational as it is enjoyable. Watching the pups interact with each other tells you about each pup's personality and place in the pack.

You should have done plenty of background homework on the Toy Manchester, and preferably have visited a few breed-club or all-breed shows, giving you an opportunity to see the breed in some numbers. This will have provide you with the chance to see the dogs with their breeders and owners, so you can give thought to which people's stock you most appreciate.

Remember that the dog you select should remain with you for the duration of his life, which is usually around 14 to 16 years, sometimes longer, so making the right decision from the outset is of utmost importance. No dog should be moved from one home to another simply because his owners were not considerate enough to have done sufficient research before selecting the breed. It is always important to remember that, when looking for a puppy, a good breeder will be assessing you as a prospective new owner just as carefully as you are selecting the breeder.

Puppies almost invariably look enchanting, but you must select one from a caring breeder who has given the puppies all of the attention they deserve and has looked after them well. It is important for breeders to socialize puppies as early as possible, and it should be apparent when you meet the litter that this has been done.

Are you ready for this black and tan bundle of love to invade your home?

PET INSURANCE

Just like you can insure your car, your house and your own health, you likewise can insure your dog's health. Investigate a pet insurance policy by talking to your vet. Depending on the age of your dog, the breed and the kind of coverage you desire, your policy can be very affordable. Most policies cover accidental injuries, poisoning and thousands of medical problems and illnesses, including cancers. Some carriers also offer routine care and immunization coverage.

The puppy you select should look well fed, but not pot-bellied, as this might indicate worms. Eyes should look bright and clear, without discharge. The nose should be moist, an indication of good health, but should never be runny. It goes without saying that there should certainly be no evidence of loose motions or parasites. The puppy you choose should also have a healthy-looking coat, an important indicator of good health internally. Any reliable Toy Manchester Terrier breeder should have health certificates from the veterinarian on all the puppies and dogs that they have for sale. If they don't, you should choose to look elsewhere.

Once you have purchased your pup, it's highly recommended that you bring him to your selected veterinarian for a thorough checkup. Be sure to inquire about the veterinarian's vaccination schedules. It's also helpful if your veterinarian is familiar with the breed itself. Many breeds of dog (the Toy Manchester Terrier included) have their own particular health concerns. Has your veterinarian worked with Manchester Terriers before? Is he or she aware of the breed's hereditary defects and other health problems? These are the types of questions you need to answer before committing yourself and your dog to a veterinarian. Your dog's veterinarian is extremely important, and finding one who is easy to work with and who understands and cares for your dog is essential. Think of it as choosing your own dentist or physician. We all have our favorites, and this is how you should choose a veterinarian. Find one that can relate to you and your pet.

Something else to consider is whether or not to take out veterinary insurance. Vet's bills can mount up, and you must always be certain that sufficient funds are available to give your dog any veterinary attention that may be needed. As insurance is becoming more popular, more types of coverage are becoming available.

BOY OR GIRL?
An important consideration to be discussed is the sex of your puppy. For a family companion, a bitch may be the better choice, considering the female's inbred concern for all young creatures and her accompanying tolerance and patience. Regardless, it is always advisable to spay or neuter your pet, which may guarantee your dog a longer life.

COMMITMENT OF OWNERSHIP

After considering all of these factors, you have most likely already made some very important decisions about selecting your puppy. You have chosen the Toy Manchester, which means that you have decided which characteristics you want in a dog and what type of dog will best fit into your family and lifestyle. If you have selected a breeder, you have gone a step further—you have done your research and found a responsible, conscientious person who breeds quality Toy Manchesters and who should be a reliable source of help as you and your puppy adjust to life together. If you have observed a litter in action, you have obtained a firsthand look at the dynamics of a puppy pack and, thus, you should have learned about each pup's individual personality—perhaps you have even found one that particularly appeals to you.

However, even if you have not yet found the Toy Manchester puppy of your dreams, observing pups will help you learn to recognize certain behavior and to determine what a pup's behavior indicates about his temperament. You will be able to pick out which pups are outgoing, confident, shy, playful, friendly, dominant, etc. Equally as important, you will learn to recognize what a healthy pup should look and act like. All of these things will help you in your search, and when you find the Toy Manchester that was meant for you, you will know it!

PUPPY APPEARANCE

Your puppy should have a well-fed appearance but not a distended abdomen, which may indicate worms or incorrect feeding, or both. The body should be firm, with a solid feel. The skin of the abdomen should be pale pink and clean, without signs of scratching or rash.

Researching your breed, selecting a responsible breeder and observing as many pups as possible are all important steps on the way to dog ownership. It may seem like a lot of effort...and you have not even taken the pup home yet! Remember, though, you cannot be too careful when it comes to deciding on the type of dog you want and finding out about your prospective pup's background. Buying a puppy is not—or *should* not be—just another whimsical purchase. This is one instance in which you actually do get to choose your own family! You may be thinking that buying a puppy should be fun—it should not be so serious and so much work. Keep in mind that your puppy is not a cuddly stuffed toy or decorative lawn ornament, but a creature that will become a real member of your family. You will come to realize that, while buying a puppy is a pleasurable and exciting endeavor, it is not something to be taken lightly. Relax...the fun will start when the pup comes home!

There's nothing a Toy Manchester enjoys more than time spent with his owner. This tiny terrier can easily share your favorite chair!

YOUR SCHEDULE . . .

If you lead an erratic, unpredictable life, with daily or weekly changes in your work requirements, consider the problems of owning a puppy. The new puppy has to be fed regularly, socialized (loved, petted, handled, introduced to other people) and, most importantly, allowed to go outdoors for house-training. As the dog gets older, he can be more tolerant of deviations in his feeding and relief schedule.

Always keep in mind that a puppy is nothing more than a baby in a puppy-dog disguise... a baby who is virtually helpless in a human world and who trusts his owner for fulfillment of his basic needs for survival.

ARE YOU PREPARED?

Unfortunately, when a puppy is bought by someone who does not take into consideration the time and attention that dog ownership requires, it is the puppy who suffers when he is either abandoned or placed in a shelter by a frustrated owner. So all of the "homework" you do in preparation for your pup's arrival will benefit you both. The more informed you are, the more you will know what to expect and the better equipped you will be to handle the ups and downs of raising a puppy. Hopefully, everyone in the household is willing to do his part in raising and caring for the pup. The anticipation of owning a dog often brings a lot of promises from excited family members: "I will walk him every day," "I will feed him," "I will housebreak him," etc., but these things take time and effort, and promises can easily be forgotten once the novelty of the new pet has worn off.

In addition to food, water and shelter, your pup needs care, protection, guidance and love. If you are not prepared to commit to this, then you are not prepared to own a dog.

"Wait a minute," you say. "How hard could this be? All of my neighbors own dogs and they seem to be doing just fine. Why should I have to worry about all of this?" Well, you should not worry about it; in fact, you will probably find that once your Toy Manchester pup gets used to his new home, he will fall into his place in the family quite naturally. But it never hurts to emphasize the commitment of dog ownership. With some time and patience, it is really not too difficult to raise a curious and exuberant Toy Manchester pup to be a well-adjusted and well-mannered adult dog—a dog that could be your most loyal friend.

PREPARING PUPPY'S PLACE IN YOUR HOME

Researching your breed and finding a breeder are only two aspects of the homework you will have to do before taking your Toy Manchester puppy home. You will also have to prepare your home and family for the new addition. Much as you would prepare a nursery for a newborn baby, you will need to designate a place in your home that will be the puppy's own. How you prepare your home will depend on how much freedom the dog will be allowed. Whatever you decide, you must ensure that he has a place that he can "call his own."

When you bring your new puppy into your home, you are bringing him into what will become his home as well. Obviously, you did not buy a puppy so that he could take control of your house, but in order for a puppy to grow into a stable, well-adjusted dog, he has to feel comfortable in his surroundings. Remember, he is leaving the warmth and security of his mother and littermates, as well as the familiarity of the only place he has ever known, so it is important to make his transition as easy as possible. By preparing a place in your home for the puppy, you are making him feel as welcome as possible in a strange new place. It should not

HANDLE WITH CARE

You should be extremely careful about handling tiny puppies. Not that you might hurt them, but that the pups' mother may exhibit what is called "maternal aggression." It is a natural, instinctive reaction for the dam to protect her young against anything she interprets as predatory or possibly harmful to her pups.

The sweetest, most gentle of bitches, after whelping a litter, often reacts this way, even to her owner.

Give your puppy a comfortable environment, but keep safety foremost in your mind. Puppies tend to eat cardboard if afforded the opportunity.

take him long to get used to it, but the sudden shock of being transplanted is somewhat traumatic for a young pup. Imagine how a small child would feel in the same situation—that is how your puppy must be feeling. It is up to you to reassure him and to let him know, "Little fellow, you are going to like it here!"

PEDIGREE VS. REGISTRATION CERTIFICATE

Too often new owners are confused between these two important documents. Your puppy's pedigree, essentially a family tree, is a written record of a dog's genealogy of three generations or more. The pedigree will show you the names as well as performance titles of all dogs in your pup's background. Your breeder must provide you with a registration application, with his part properly filled out. You must complete the application and send it to the AKC with the proper fee. Every puppy must come from a litter that has been AKC-registered by the breeder, born in the USA and from a sire and dam that are also registered with the AKC.

The seller must provide you with complete records to identify the puppy. The AKC requires that the seller provide the buyer with the following: breed; sex, color and markings; date of birth; litter number (when available); names and registration numbers of the parents; breeder's name; and date sold or delivered.

WHAT YOU SHOULD BUY

CRATE

To someone unfamiliar with the use of crates in dog training, it may seem like punishment to shut a dog in a crate, but this is not the case at all. More and more breeders and trainers around the world are recommending crates as preferred tools for pet puppies as well as show puppies. Crates are not cruel—crates have many humane and highly effective uses in dog care and training. For example, crate training is a very popular and very successful house-training method. A crate can keep your dog safe during travel and, perhaps most importantly, a crate provides

ARE YOU A FIT OWNER?
If the breeder from whom you are buying a puppy asks you a lot of personal questions, do not be insulted. Such a breeder wants to be sure that you will be a fit provider for his puppy.

your dog with a place of his own in your home. It serves as a "doggie bedroom" of sorts—your Toy Manchester can curl up in his crate when he wants to sleep or when he just needs a break. Many dogs sleep in their crates overnight. With soft bedding and his favorite toy, a crate becomes a cozy pseudo-den for your dog. Like his ancestors, he too will seek out the comfort and retreat of a den—you just happen to be providing him with something a little more

PHOTO COURTESY OF DOSKOCIL.

Visit your local pet shop to see the selection of crates available. A small wire or fiberglass (pictured) crate will be suitable for your Toy Manchester Terrier.

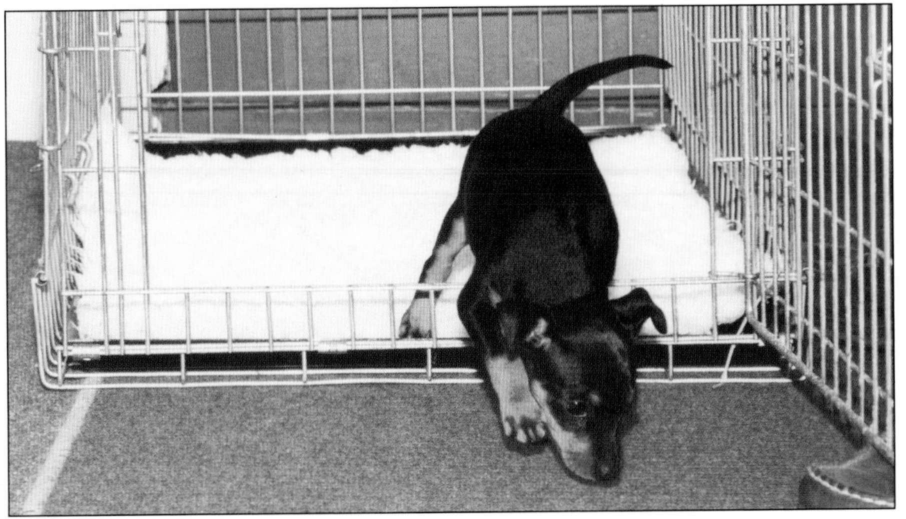

You should acclimate your new Toy Manchester Terrier to his crate as soon as you bring him home. The wire crate is best for use in the home, as it gives the puppy good visibility and ventilation.

Breeders commonly begin to house-train the litter by using newspaper around the puppies' sleeping area. A setup like this teaches the puppy cleanliness and structure, two essentials of canine living.

luxurious than what his early ancestors enjoyed.

As far as purchasing a crate, the type that you buy is up to you. It will most likely be one of the two most popular types: wire or fiberglass. There are advantages and disadvantages to each type. For example, a wire crate is more open, allowing the air to flow through and affording the dog a view of what is going on around him while a fiberglass crate is sturdier. Both can double as travel crates, providing protection for the dog in the car. A small crate should be fine for a Toy Manchester as a pup and adult, as the breed is handily one of the smallest in the dog world.

STRESS-FREE

Some experts in canine health advise that stress during a dog's early years of development can compromise and weaken his immune system, and may trigger the potential for a shortened life. They emphasize the need for happy and stress-free growing-up years.

Bedding

A nice crate pad and a blanket in the dog's crate will help the dog feel more at home. These will take the place of the leaves, twigs, etc., that the pup would use in the wild to make a den; the pup can make his own "burrow" in the crate. Although your pup is far removed from his den-making ancestors, the denning instinct is still a part of his genetic makeup. Second, until you take your pup home, he has been sleeping amid the warmth of his dam and littermates, and while a blanket is not the same as a warm, breathing body, it still provides heat and something with which to snuggle. You will want to wash your pup's bedding frequently in case he has an accident in his crate, and replace or remove any pad or blanket that becomes ragged and starts to fall apart.

Toys

Toys are a must for dogs of all ages, especially for curious playful pups. Puppies are the children of the dog world, and what child does not love toys? Chew toys provide enjoyment for both dog and owner—your dog will enjoy playing with his favorite toys, while you will enjoy the fact that they distract him from your expensive shoes and leather sofa. Puppies love to chew; in fact, chewing is a phys-

TOYS, TOYS, TOYS!

With a big variety of dog toys available, and so many that look like they would be a lot of fun for a dog, be careful in your selection. It is amazing what a set of puppy teeth can do to an innocent-looking toy, so, obviously, safety is a major consideration. Be sure to choose the most durable products that you can find. Hard nylon bones and toys are a safe bet, and many of them are offered in different scents and flavors that will be sure to capture your dog's attention. It is always fun to play a game of fetch with your dog, and there are balls and flying discs that are specially made to withstand dog teeth.

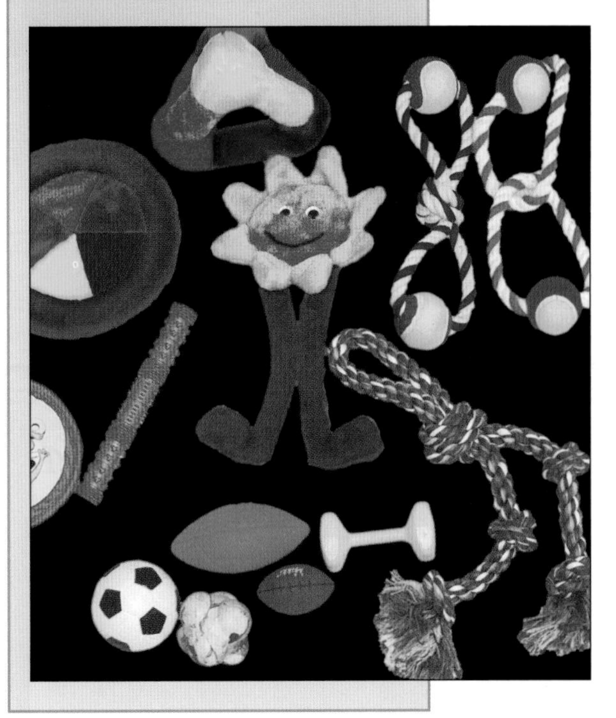

Your local pet shop should have a wide array of leads from which you can choose one that suits your Toy Manchester.

ical need for pups as they are teething, and everything looks appetizing! The full range of your possessions—from your favorite slipper to your new Persian carpet—are fair game in the eyes of a teething pup. Puppies are not all that discerning when it comes to finding something to literally "sink their teeth into"—everything tastes great!

Choose chew toys that are safe without any potentially harmful parts. Always take care when giving squeaky toys, for Toy Manchesters will usually remove squeaks and eyes immediately! If a pup "disembowels" one of these, the small plastic squeaker inside can be dangerous if swallowed. Monitor the condition of all of your pup's toys carefully and get rid of any that have been chewed to the point of becoming potentially dangerous.

Some breeders advise owners to resist stuffed toys, because they can become de-stuffed in no time. The overly excited pup may ingest the stuffing, which is neither nutritious nor digestible. Be careful of natural bones, which have a tendency to splinter into sharp, dangerous pieces.

FINANCIAL RESPONSIBILITY

Grooming tools, collars, leashes, crates, dog beds and, of course, toys will be expenses to you when you first obtain your pup, and the cost will continue throughout your dog's lifetime. If your puppy damages or destroys your possessions (as most puppies surely will!) or something belonging to a neighbor, you can calculate additional expense. There is also flea and pest control, which every dog owner faces more than once. You must be able to handle the financial responsibility of owning a dog.

Also be careful of rawhide, which can turn into pieces that are easy to swallow and become a mushy mess on your carpet.

LEASH

A nylon leash is probably the best option as it is the most resistant to puppy teeth should your pup take a liking to chewing on his leash. Of course, this is a habit that should be nipped in the bud, but, if your pup likes to chew on his leash, he has a very slim chance of being able to chew through the strong nylon. Nylon leashes are also lightweight, which is good for a young Toy Manchester who is just getting used to the idea of walking on a leash. For everyday walking and safety purposes, the nylon leash is a good choice. As your pup grows up and gets used

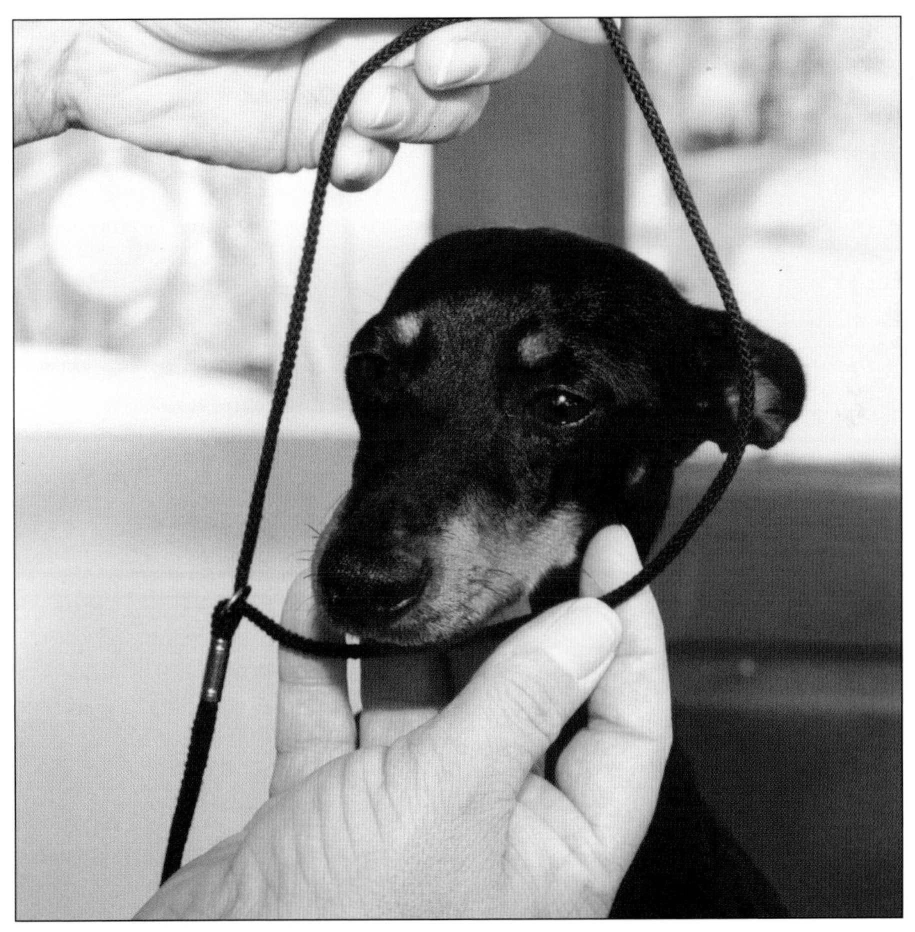

A sturdy nylon or cotton collar is a good lightweight choice for training and showing a Toy Manchester.

Your local pet shop will have suitable food and water bowls. Your Toy Manchester will not require large bowls, and choose bowls that are durable and easy to clean.

PHOTO COURTESY OF MIKKI PET PRODUCTS.

to walking on the leash, you may want to purchase a flexible leash. These leashes allow you to extend the length to give the dog a broader area to explore or to shorten the length to keep the dog near you.

COLLAR

Your pup should get used to wearing a collar all the time since you will want to attach his ID tags to it. Plus, you have to attach the leash to something! A lightweight nylon collar is a good choice; make sure that it fits snugly enough so that the pup cannot wriggle out of it, but is loose enough so that it will not be uncomfortably tight around the pup's neck. You should be able to fit a finger between the pup and the collar. It may take some time for your pup to get used to wearing the collar, but soon he will not even notice that it is there.

Choke collars are made for training, but are not suitable for the Toy Manchester or any Toy breed. Many toy-breed owners prefer to use harnesses on their dogs, as these give the owner better control and the dog feels more comfortable without a collar around his tiny neck.

FOOD AND WATER BOWLS

Your pup will need two bowls, one for food and one for water. You may want two sets of bowls,

CHOOSE AN APPROPRIATE COLLAR

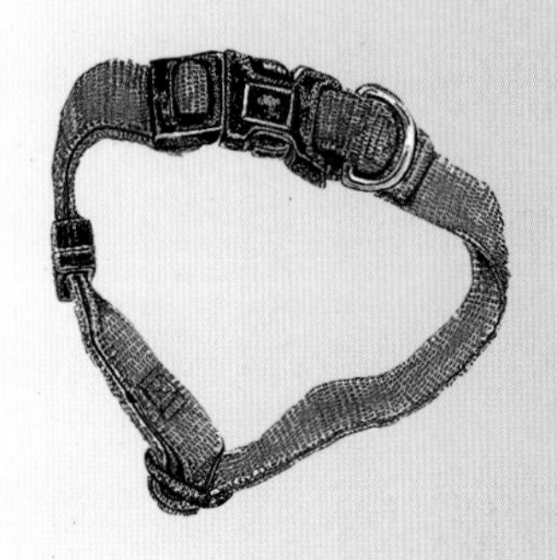

The **BUCKLE COLLAR** is the standard collar used for everyday purposes. Be sure that you adjust the buckle on growing puppies. Check it every day. It can become too tight overnight! These collars can be made of leather or nylon. Attach your dog's identification tags to this collar.

The **CHOKE COLLAR** is designed for training. It is constructed of highly polished steel so that it slides easily through the stainless steel loop. The idea is that the dog controls the pressure around his neck and he will stop pulling if the collar becomes uncomfortable. It should *not* be used on a Toy Manchester Terrier.

The **HALTER** is for a trained dog that has to be restrained to prevent running away, chasing a cat and the like. Considered the most humane of all collars, it is frequently used on smaller dogs on which collars are not comfortable.

one for inside and one for outside, depending on where the dog will be fed and where he will be spending time. Stainless steel or sturdy plastic bowls are popular choices. Plastic bowls are more chewable. Dogs tend not to chew on the steel variety, which can be sterilized. It is important to buy sturdy bowls since anything is in danger of being chewed by puppy teeth and you do not want your dog to be constantly chewing apart his bowl (for his safety and for your wallet!).

Owning a dog means cleaning up after him. Tools like this make the task less of a chore.

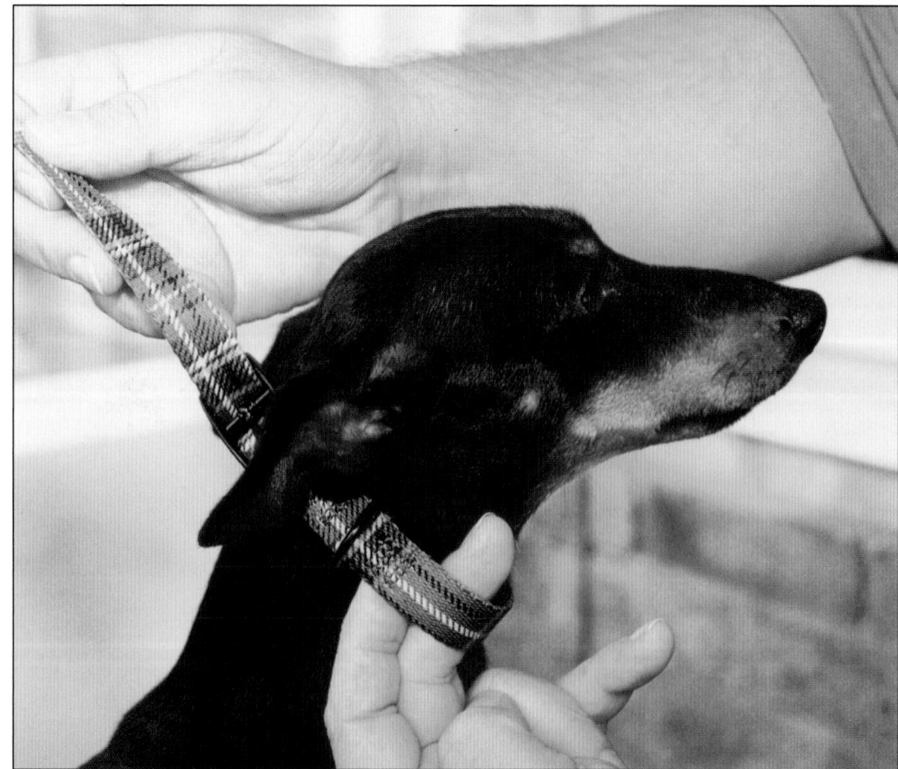

Pet shops have many varieties of collars suitable for a Toy Manchester Terrier. Purchase an appropriately sized collar, keeping in mind that the puppy will grow and you'll need to adjust the size accordingly.

Cleaning Supplies

Until a pup is house-trained, you will be doing a lot of cleaning. "Accidents" will occur, which is acceptable in the beginning because the puppy does not know any better. All you can do is be prepared to clean up any accidents. Old rags, towels, newspapers and a safe disinfectant are good to have on hand.

Beyond the Basics

The items previously discussed are the bare necessities. You will find out what else you need as you go along—grooming supplies, flea/tick protection, baby gates to partition a room, etc. These things will vary depending on your situation, but it is important that you have everything you need to feed and make your Toy Manchester comfortable in his first few days at home.

PUPPY-PROOFING YOUR HOME

Aside from making sure that your Toy Manchester will be comfortable in your home, you also have to make sure that your home is safe for your Toy Manchester. This means taking precautions that your pup will not get into anything he should not get into and that there is nothing within his reach that may harm him should he sniff it, chew it, inspect it, etc. This probably seems obvious since, while you are primarily concerned with your pup's safety, at the same time you do not want your belongings to be ruined. Breakables should be placed out of reach if your dog is to have full run of the house.

TEETHING TIP

Puppies like soft toys for chewing. Because they are teething, soft items like stuffed toys soothe their aching gums, but be sure to monitor your pup when he's playing with a potentially destructible (and thus potentially dangerous) toy.

PLAY'S THE THING

Teaching the puppy to play with his toys in running and fetching games is an ideal way to help the puppy develop muscle, learn motor skills and bond with you, his owner and master. He also needs to learn how to inhibit his bite reflex and never to use his teeth on people, forbidden objects and other animals in play. Whenever you play with your puppy, you make the rules. This becomes an important message to your puppy in teaching him that you are the pack leader and control everything he does in life. Once your dog accepts you as his leader, your relationship with him will be cemented for life.

If he is to be limited to certain places within the house, keep any potentially dangerous items in the "off-limits" areas. An electrical cord can pose a danger should the puppy decide to taste it—and who is going to convince a pup that it would not make a great chew toy? Cords should be fastened tightly against the wall, out of the reach of the puppy. If your dog is going to spend time in a crate, make sure that there is nothing near his crate that he can reach if he sticks his curious little nose or paws through the openings. Just as you would with a child, keep all household cleaners and chemicals where the pup cannot reach them.

It is also important to make sure that the outside of your home is safe. Of course your puppy should never be unsupervised, but a pup let loose in the yard will want to run and explore, and he should be granted that freedom. Do not let a fence give you a false sense of security; you would be surprised how crafty (and persistent) a dog can be in working out how to dig under and squeeze his way through small holes, or to climb over a fence. Lest we regret that we forgot, the Toy Manchester Terrier derives from "digging earthdogs," and can be quite determined in his excavation habits.

The remedy is to make the fence well embedded into the ground and high enough so that it really is impossible for your dog to get over it (about 5 feet should suffice). Be sure to secure any gaps in the fence. Check the fence periodically to ensure that it is in good shape and make repairs as needed; a very determined pup may return to the same spot to "work on it" until he is able to get through.

FIRST TRIP TO THE VET

You have selected your puppy, and your home and family are ready. Now all you have to do is collect your Toy Manchester from the breeder and the fun begins, right? Well...not so fast. Something else you need to prepare is your pup's first trip to the vet. Perhaps the breeder can recommend someone in the area who specializes in small breeds, or maybe you know some other Toy Manchester owners who can suggest a good vet. Either way, you should have

Never underestimate the power of food. Most puppies will respond enthusiastically to a food treat in training.

MENTAL AND DENTAL

Toys not only help your puppy get the physical and mental stimulation he needs but also provide a great way to keep his teeth clean. Hard rubber or nylon toys, especially those constructed with grooves, are designed to scrape away plaque, preventing bad breath and gum infection.

an appointment arranged for your pup before you pick him up.

The pup's first visit will consist of an overall examination to make sure that the pup does not have any problems that are not apparent to you. The vet will also set up a schedule for the pup's vaccinations; the breeder will inform you of which ones the pup has already received and the vet can continue from there.

FEEDING TIPS

You will probably start feeding your pup the same food that he has been getting from the breeder; the breeder should give you a few days' supply to start you off. Although you should not give your pup too many treats, you will want to have puppy treats on hand for coaxing, training, rewards, etc. Be careful, though, as a small pup's calorie requirements are relatively low and a few treats can add up to almost a full day's worth of calories without the required nutrition.

INTRODUCTION TO THE FAMILY

Everyone in the house will be excited about the puppy's coming home and will want to pet him and play with him, but it is best to make the introductions low-key so as not to overwhelm the puppy. He is apprehensive already. It is the first time he has been separated from his dam and the breeder, and the ride to your home is likely to be the first time he has been in a car. The last thing you want to do is smother him, as this will only frighten him further. This is not to say that human contact is not extremely necessary at this stage, because this is the time when a connection between the pup and his human family is formed. Gentle petting and soothing words should help console him, as well as just putting him down and letting him explore on his own (under your watchful eye, of course).

The pup may approach the family members or may busy himself with exploring for a while. Gradually, each person should spend some time with the pup, one at a time, crouching down to get as close to the

Nip puppy problems in the bud. Puppy teeth can hardly tear your leather moccasins, but adult teeth will make rawhide of them!

pup's level as possible and letting him sniff their hands and petting him gently. He definitely needs human attention and he needs to be touched—this is how to form an immediate bond. Just remember that the pup is experiencing a lot of things for the first time, at the same time. There are new people, new noises, new smells and new things to investigate, so be gentle, be affectionate and be as comforting as you can be.

HOW VACCINES WORK

If you've just bought a puppy, you surely know the importance of having your pup vaccinated, but do you understand how vaccines work? Vaccines contain the same bacteria or viruses that cause the disease you want to prevent, but they have been chemically modified so that they don't cause any harm. Instead, the vaccine causes your dog to produce antibodies that fight the harmful bacteria. Thus, if your dog is exposed to the disease in the future, the antibodies will destroy the viruses or bacteria.

Owners must provide suitable fencing for their Toy Manchesters. They can easily climb formidable fences, as can be seen in this series of photos. Select fencing that cannot be climbed, at least 5 feet high so that it cannot be scaled or jumped.

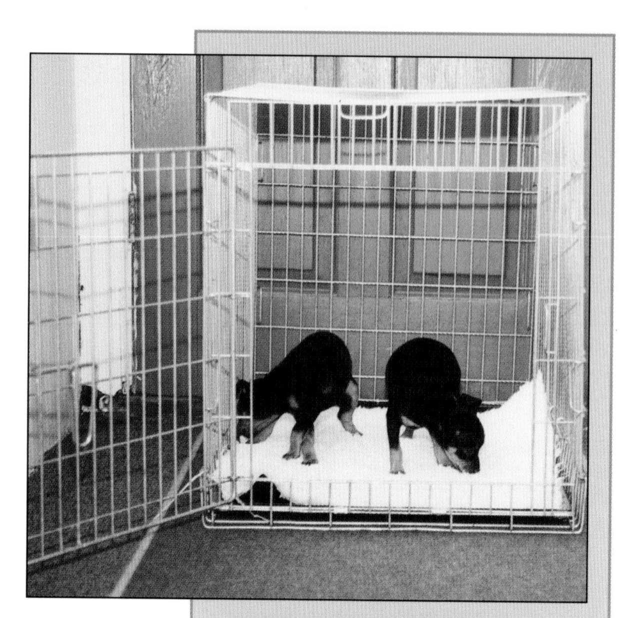

CRATE-TRAINING TIPS

During crate training, you should partition off the section of the crate in which the pup stays. If he is given too big an area, this will hinder your training efforts. Crate training is based on the fact that a dog does not like to soil his sleeping quarters, so it is ineffective to keep a pup in an area that is so big that he can eliminate in one end and get far enough away from it to sleep. Also, you want to make the crate den-like for the pup. Blankets and a favorite toy will make the crate cozy for the small pup; as he grows, you may want to evict some of his "roommates" to make more room. It will take some coaxing at first, but be patient. Given some time to get used to it, your pup will adapt to his new home-within-a-home quite nicely.

PUP'S FIRST NIGHT HOME

You have traveled home with your new charge safely in his crate or a friend or family member's lap. He's been to the vet for a thorough check-up; he's been weighed, his papers examined; perhaps he's even been vaccinated and wormed as well. He's met the family and licked the whole family, including the excited children and the less-than-happy cat. He's explored his area, his new bed, the yard and anywhere else he's been permitted. He's eaten his first meal at home and relieved himself in the proper place. He's heard lots of new sounds, smelled new friends and seen more of the outside world than ever before.

That was just the first day! He's worn out and is ready for bed...or so you think!

It's puppy's first night and you are ready to say "Good night"—keep in mind that this is puppy's first night ever to be sleeping alone. His dam and littermates are no longer at paw's length and he's a bit scared, cold and lonely. Be reassuring to your new family member, but this is not the time to spoil him and give in to his inevitable whining.

Puppies whine. They whine to let others know where they are and hopefully to get company out of it. Place your pup in his new bed or crate in his room and close the crate door. Mercifully, he may fall asleep without a peep. When the inevitable occurs, ignore the whining: he is fine. Be strong and keep his interest in mind. Do not allow yourself to feel guilty and visit the pup. He will fall asleep eventually.

Many breeders recommend placing a piece of bedding from his former home in his new bed so that he recognizes the scent of his littermates. Others still advise placing a hot water bottle in his bed for warmth. This latter may be a good idea provided the pup doesn't attempt to suckle—he'll get good and wet and may not fall asleep so fast.

Puppy's first night can be somewhat stressful for the pup and his new family. Remember that you are setting the tone of nighttime at your house. Unless you want to play with your pup every night at 10 p.m., midnight and 2 a.m., don't initiate the habit. Your family will thank you, and eventually so will your pup!

Your Toy Manchester puppy's first day at your home will be exciting and exhausting. Your puppy may not be nearly as tired as you are when twilight comes!

NATURAL TOXINS

Examine your grass and landscaping before bringing your puppy home. Many varieties of plants have leaves, stems or flowers that are toxic if ingested, and you can depend on a curious puppy to investigate them. Ask your vet for information on poisonous plants or research them at your library.

If you see your dog carrying a piece of vegetation in his mouth, approach him in a quiet, disinterested manner, avoid eye contact, pet him and gradually remove the plant from his mouth. Alternatively, offer him a treat and maybe he'll drop the plant on his own accord. Be sure no toxic plants are growing in your own yard or kept in your home.

THE COCOA WARS

Chocolate contains the chemical thebromine, which is poisonous to dogs, although "chocolates" especially made for dogs are safe (as they don't actually contain chocolate) but not recommended. Any item that encourages your dog to enjoy the taste of cocoa should be discouraged. You should also exercise caution when using mulch in your yard or garden. This frequently contains cocoa hulls, and dogs have been known to die from eating the mulch.

PREVENTING PUPPY PROBLEMS

Socialization

Now that you have done all of the preparatory work and have helped your pup get accustomed to his new home and family, it is about time for you to have some fun! Socializing your Toy Manchester pup gives you the opportunity to show off your new friend, and your pup gets to reap the benefits of being an adorable little creature that people will want to pet and, in general, think is absolutely precious!

Besides getting to know his new family, your puppy should be exposed to other people, animals and situations, but of course he must not come into close contact with dogs you don't know well until his course of injections is fully complete. Socialization will help him become well adjusted as he grows up and less prone to being timid or fearful of the new things he will encounter. Your pup's socialization began with the breeder, but now it is your responsibility to continue it. The socialization he receives up until the age of 12 weeks is the most critical, as this is the time when he forms his impressions of the outside world. Be especially careful if you have your puppy during the eight-to-ten-week-old period, also known as the fear period. The interaction he receives during this time should be gentle and reassuring. Lack of socialization can manifest itself in fear and aggression as the dog grows up. He needs lots of human contact, affection, handling and exposure to other animals.

Once your pup has received his necessary vaccinations, feel free to take him out and about (on his leash, of course). Walk him around the neighborhood, take him on your daily errands, let people pet him, let him meet other dogs and pets, etc. Puppies do not have to try to make friends; there will be no shortage of people who will want to introduce themselves. Just make sure that you care-

CHEMICAL TOXINS

Scour your garage for potential puppy dangers. Remove weed killers, pesticides and antifreeze materials. Antifreeze is highly toxic and just a few drops can kill a puppy or an adult dog. The sweet taste attracts the animal, who will quickly consume it from the floor or pavement.

fully supervise each meeting. If the neighborhood children want to say hello, for example, that is great—children and pups most often make great companions. However, sometimes an excited child can unintentionally handle a pup too roughly, or an overzealous pup can playfully nip a little too hard. You want to make socialization experiences positive ones. What a pup learns during this very formative stage will affect his attitude toward future encounters. You want your dog to be comfortable around everyone. A pup that has a bad experience with a child may grow up to be a dog that is shy around or aggressive toward children.

Consistency in Training

Dogs, being pack animals, naturally need a leader, or else they try to establish dominance in their packs. When you welcome a dog into your family, the choice of who becomes the leader and who becomes the pack is entirely up to you! Your pup's intuitive quest for dominance, coupled with the fact that it is nearly impossible to look at an adorable Toy Manchester pup with his puppy-dog eyes and not cave in give the pup almost an unfair

Exploring his new digs is a genuine adventure for the tiny Toy Manchester. You must supervise your puppy constantly whenever he is exploring around the house.

advantage in getting the upper hand! A pup will definitely test the waters to see what he can and cannot do.

Do not give in to those pleading eyes—stand your ground when it comes to disciplining the pup and make sure that all family members do the same. It will only confuse the pup when Mother tells him to get off the sofa when he is used to sitting up there with Father to watch the nightly news. Avoid discrepancies by having all members of the household decide on the rules before the pup even comes home...and be consistent in enforcing them! Early training shapes the dog's personality, so you cannot be unclear in what you expect.

PUPPY PROBLEMS

The majority of problems that are commonly seen in young pups will disappear as your dog gets older. However, how you deal with problems when he is young will determine how he reacts to discipline as an adult dog. It is important to establish who is boss (hopefully it will be you!) right away when you are first bonding with your dog. This bond will set the tone for the rest of your life together.

COMMON PUPPY PROBLEMS

The best way to prevent puppy problems is to be proactive in stopping an undesirable behavior as soon as it starts. The old saying "You can't teach an old dog new tricks" does not necessarily hold true, but it *is* true that it is much easier to discourage bad behavior in a young developing pup than to wait until the pup's bad behavior becomes the adult dog's bad habit. There are some problems that are especially prevalent in puppies as they develop.

NIPPING

As puppies start to teethe, they feel the need to sink their teeth into anything available...unfortunately that includes your fingers, arms, hair and toes. You may find this behavior cute for the first five seconds...until you feel just how sharp those puppy

Toy Manchester Terriers easily socialize with children. Toddlers must never be allowed to be alone with a dog for the safety of both parties.

MANNERS MATTER

During the socialization process, a puppy should meet people, experience different environments and definitely be exposed to other canines. Through playing and interacting with other dogs, your puppy will learn lessons, ranging from controlling the pressure of his jaws by biting his littermates to the inner-workings of the canine pack that he will apply to his human relationships for the rest of his life. That is why removing a puppy from his litter too early (before eight weeks) can be detrimental to the pup's development.

teeth are. This is something you want to discourage immediately and consistently with a firm "No!" (or whatever number of firm "Nos" it takes for him to understand that you mean business). Then replace your finger with an appropriate chew toy. While this behavior is merely annoying when the dog is young, it can become dangerous as your Toy Manchester's adult teeth grow in and his jaws develop, and he continues to think it is okay to gnaw on human appendages. Your Toy Manchester does not mean any harm with a friendly nip, but he also does not know his own strength.

Crying/Whining

Your pup will often cry, whine, whimper, howl or make some type of commotion when he is left alone. This is basically his way of calling out for attention to make sure that you know he is there and that you have not forgotten about him. He feels insecure when he is left alone, when you are out of the house and he is in his crate or when you are in another part of the house and he cannot see you. The noise he is making is an expression of the anxiety he feels at being alone, so he needs to be taught that being alone is okay. You are not actually training the dog to stop making

No bull! Toy Manchester Terriers are eager and alert students who enjoy quality time with their owners.

noise, you are training him to feel comfortable when he is alone and thus removing the need for him to make the noise. This is where the crate with cozy bedding and a toy comes in handy. You want to know that he is safe when you are not there to supervise, and you know that he will be safe in his crate rather than roaming freely about the house. In order for the pup to stay in his crate without making a fuss, he needs to be

TRAINING TIP

Training your puppy takes much patience and can be frustrating at times, but you should see results from your efforts. If you have a puppy that seems untrainable, take him to a trainer or behaviorist. The dog may have a personality problem that requires the help of a professional, or perhaps you need help in learning how to train your dog.

CHEWING TIPS

Chewing goes hand in hand with nipping in the sense that a teething puppy is always looking for a way to soothe his aching gums. In this case, instead of chewing on you, he may have taken a liking to your favorite shoe or something else that he should not be chewing. Again, realize that this is a normal canine behavior that does not need to be discouraged, only redirected. Your pup just needs to be taught what is acceptable to chew on and what is off-limits. Consistently tell him "No!" when you catch him chewing on something forbidden and give him a chew toy.

Conversely, praise him when you catch him chewing on something appropriate. In this way, you are discouraging the inappropriate behavior and reinforcing the desired behavior. The puppy's chewing should stop after his adult teeth have come in, but an adult dog continues to chew for various reasons—perhaps because he is bored, needs to relieve tension or just likes to chew. That is why it is important to redirect his chewing when he is still young.

comfortable in his crate. On that note, it is extremely important that the crate is never used as a form of punishment, or the pup will have a negative association with the crate.

Accustom the pup to the crate in short, gradually increasing time intervals in which you put him in the crate, maybe with a treat, and stay in the room with him. If he cries or makes a fuss, do not go to him, but stay in his sight. Gradually he will realize that staying in his crate is all right without your help, and it will not be so traumatic for him when you are not around. You may want to leave the radio on softly when you leave the house; the sound of human voices may be comforting to him.

EVERYDAY CARE OF YOUR

TOY MANCHESTER TERRIER

DIETARY AND FEEDING CONSIDERATIONS

Today the choices of food for your Toy Manchester are many and varied. There are simply dozens of brands of food in all sorts of flavors and textures, ranging from puppy diets to those for seniors. There are even hypoallergenic and low-calorie diets available. Because your Toy Manchester's food has a bearing on coat, health and temperament, it is essential that the most suitable diet is selected for a Toy Manchester of his age. It is fair to say, however, that even experienced owners can be perplexed by the enormous range of foods available. Only understanding what is best for your dog will help you reach an informed decision.

Dog foods are produced in three basic types: dry, semi-moist and canned. Dry foods are useful for the cost-conscious, for overall they tend to be less expensive than semi-moist or canned. Dry foods also contain the least fat and the most preservatives. In general, canned foods are made up of 60–70% water, while semi-moist ones often contain so much sugar that they are perhaps the least preferred by owners, even though their dogs seem to like them.

When selecting your dog's diet, three stages of development

STORING DOG FOOD

You must store your dry dog food carefully. Open packages of dog food quickly lose their vitamin value, usually within 90 days of being opened. Mold spores and vermin could also contaminate the food.

must be considered: the puppy stage, the adult stage and the senior stage.

Puppy Diets

Puppies instinctively want to suck milk from their mother's teats and a normal puppy will exhibit this behavior from just a few moments following birth. If puppies do not attempt to suckle within the first half-hour or so, the breeder should encourage them to do so by placing them on the nipples, having selected ones with plenty of milk. This early milk supply is important in providing colostrum to protect the puppies during the first eight to ten weeks of their lives. Although a mother's milk is much better than any milk formula, despite there being some excellent ones available, if the puppies do not feed, the breeder will have to hand-feed them. For those with less experience, advice from a vet is important so that not only the right quantity of milk is fed but also that of correct quality, fed at suitably frequent intervals, usually every two hours during the first few days of life.

Puppies should be allowed to nurse from their dam for about the first six weeks, although from the third or fourth week the breeder will begin to introduce small portions of suitable solid food. Most breeders like to introduce alternate milk and meat meals initially, building up to weaning time.

By the time the puppies are seven or a maximum of eight weeks old, they should be fully weaned and fed solely on a proprietary puppy food. Selection of the most suitable, good-quality diet at this time is essential, for a puppy's fastest growth rate is during the first year of life. Vets and breeders are able to offer advice in this regard. The frequency of meals will be reduced over time, and when a young dog has reached the age of about 15 months, an adult diet can be fed.

Puppy and junior diets should be well balanced for the needs of your dog, so that, except in

TIPPING THE SCALES

Good nutrition is vital to your dog's health, but many people end up overfeeding or giving unnecessary supplements. Here are some common doggie diet don'ts:

- Adding milk, yogurt and cheese to your dog's diet may seem like a good idea for coat and skin care, but dairy products are very fattening and can cause indigestion.
- Diets high in fat will not cause heart attacks in dogs but will certainly cause your dog to gain weight.
- Most importantly, don't assume your dog will simply stop eating once he doesn't need any more food. Given the chance, he will eat you out of house and home!

THE CANINE GOURMET

Your dog does not prefer a fresh bone. Indeed, he wants it properly aged and, if given such a treat indoors, he is more likely to try to bury it in the carpet than he is to settle in for a good chew! If you have a yard, give him such delicacies outside and guide him to a place suitable for his "bone yard." He will carefully place the treasure in its earthy vault and seemingly forget about it. Trust me, his seeming distaste or lack of thanks for your thoughtfulness is not that at all. He will return in a few days to inspect the bone, perhaps to re-bury it, and when it is just right, he will relish it as much as you do that cooked-to-perfection steak. If he is in a concrete or bricked kennel run, he will be especially frustrated at the hopelessness of the situation. He will vacillate between ignoring it completely, giving it a few licks to speed the curing process with saliva, and trying to hide it behind the water bowl! When the bone has aged a bit, he will set to work on it.

certain circumstances, additional vitamins, minerals and proteins will not be required.

ADULT DIETS

A dog is considered an adult when he has stopped growing. Although the Toy Manchester continues to develop physically until around three years of age, in general the breeder's diet can be changed to an adult one at about 15 months of age. Again you should rely upon your vet or breeder to recommend an acceptable adult-maintenance diet. Major dog-food manufacturers specialize in this type of food, and it is merely necessary for you to select the one best suited to your dog's needs. Active dogs may have different requirements than more sedate dogs.

SENIOR DIETS

As dogs get older, their metabolism changes. The older dog usually exercises less, moves more slowly and sleeps more. This change in lifestyle and physiological performance requires a change in diet. Since these changes take place slowly, they might not be recognizable. What is easily recognizable is weight gain. By continuing to feed your dog an adult-maintenance diet when he is

Toy Manchester puppies have a keen sense of smell. Be careful, though, as their noses lead them toward trouble.

FEEDING TIPS

- Dog food must be served at room temperature, neither too hot nor too cold. Fresh water, changed often and served in a clean bowl, is mandatory, especially when feeding dry food.
- Never feed your dog from the table while you are eating, and never feed your dog leftovers from your own meal. They usually contain too much fat and too much seasoning.
- Dogs must chew their food. Hard pellets are excellent; soups and stews are to be avoided.
- Don't add leftovers or any extras to commercial dog food. The normal food is usually balanced, and adding something extra destroys the balance.
- Except for age-related changes, dogs do not require dietary variations. They can be fed the same diet, day after day, without their becoming bored or ill.

slowing down metabolically, your dog will gain weight. Obesity in an older dog compounds the health problems that already accompany old age.

As your dog gets older, few of his organs function up to par. The kidneys slow down and the intestines become less efficient. These age-related factors are best handled with a change in diet and a change in feeding schedule to give smaller portions that are more easily digested.

There is no single best diet for every older dog. While many dogs do well on light or senior diets, other dogs do better on puppy diets or special premium diets such as lamb and rice. Be sensitive to your senior Toy Manchester's diet and this will help control other problems that may arise with your old friend.

WATER

Just as your dog needs proper nutrition from his food, water is

"What's for supper?" Dining may well be your Toy Manchester's favorite activity. This is a discerning dinner companion who deserves the finest.

Clean, fresh water should always be available outdoors for your Toy Manchester so that he can have a cool drink when playing or exercising.

an essential "nutrient" as well. Water keeps the dog's body properly hydrated and promotes normal function of the body's systems. During housebreaking, it is necessary to keep an eye on how much water your Toy Manchester is drinking, but once he is reliably trained he should have access to clean, fresh water at all times, especially if you feed dry food. Make certain that the dog's water bowl is clean, and change the water often.

EXERCISE

The Toy Manchester is an active dog that enjoys daily exercise with his owner. Given the small size of the breed, the exercise regimen is not so demanding that any owner cannot meet its requirements. Most Toy Manchesters will accept as much exercise as they are given, but welcome at least two daily walks and some off-leash running time (in a safely fenced area, of course).

After exercise, they should be

DRINK, DRANK, DRUNK—MAKE IT A DOUBLE

In both humans and dogs, as well as other living organisms, water forms the major part of nearly every body tissue. Naturally, we take water for granted, but without it, life as we know it would cease.

For dogs, water is needed to keep their bodies functioning biochemically. Additionally, water is needed to replace the water lost while panting. Unlike humans, who are able to sweat to dissipate heat, dogs must pant to cool down, thereby losing the vital water that their bodies need to regulate their body temperatures. Humans lose electrolyte-containing products and other body-fluid components through sweating; dogs do not lose anything except water.

Water is essential always, but especially so when the weather is hot or humid or when your dog is exercising or working vigorously.

allowed to settle down quietly for a rest, and please remember that following exercise, at least one full hour should always be allowed before feeding. Puppies should have only limited exercise during the crucial period of bone growth, so young dogs should be exercised with care.

Because Toy Manchesters can be gifted excavators, it goes without saying that the yard must be completely dog-proof, and the perimeters must be checked regularly to be sure your Toy Manchester is not working on new exit route, likely by means of digging or chewing through a fence. It does not take a very large hole for a Toy Manchester to escape.

GROOMING AND BATHING

Toy Manchesters need little grooming and are generally clean dogs, virtually free from doggy odors. Bathing is only needed occasionally and, when selecting a shampoo, take into consideration that some Toy Manchesters have a reaction to insecticides. If ever a product used on the coat causes skin irritation, stop using it immediately and change to one that is milder.

Even when showing a Toy Manchester, little grooming is required. A light brush (not metal or wire) or a rubber or sisal mitt will remove dead hair, then go over the coat with a hound glove to put the finishing touch. Hound gloves do vary, but a useful type is chamois leather on one side and velvet on the other. A good wipe-over with the chamois side, and then with the velvet side, produces a nice sheen on the coat and is good stimulation for the skin. In between baths, it can be

Competition around the feeding bowl entices the litter's appetite. Once your Toy Manchester Terrier comes home, he may need a little encouragement to eat his whole meal with gusto.

CHANGE IN DIET

As your dog's caretaker, you know the importance of keeping his diet consistent, but sometimes when you run out of food or if you're on vacation, you have to make a change quickly. Some dogs will experience digestive problems, but most will not. If you are planning on changing your dog's menu, do so gradually to ensure that your dog will not have any problems. Over a period of four to five days, slowly add some new food to your dog's old food, increasing the percentage of new food each day.

Your local pet shop can easily supply the few grooming tools needed to keep your Toy Manchester Terrier's coat in prime condition.

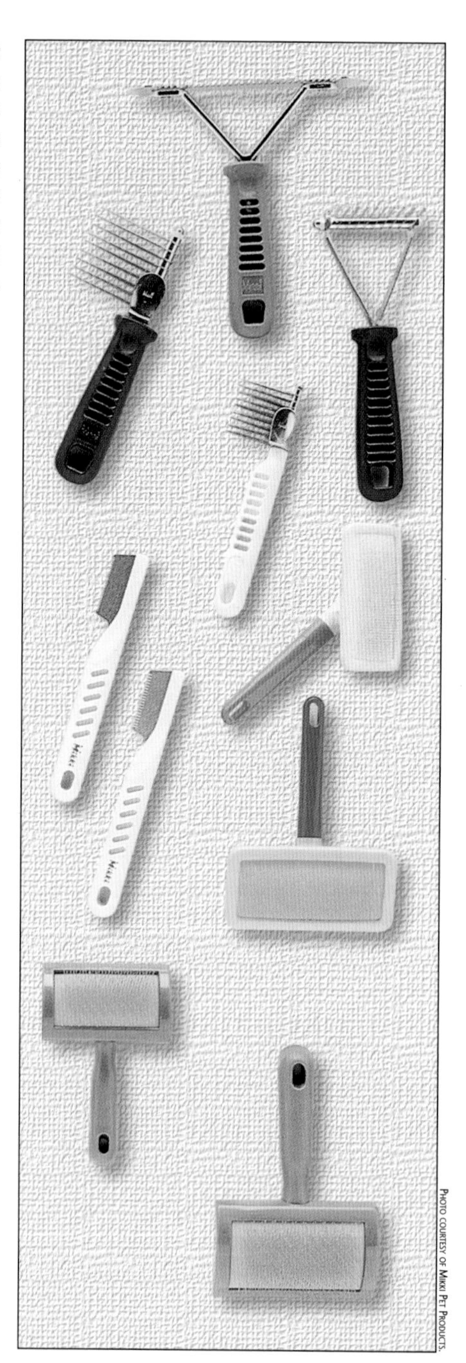

PHOTO COURTESY OF MIKKI PET PRODUCTS.

GROOMING EQUIPMENT

Invest in quality grooming tools that will last you and your Toy Manchester for many years of use. Here are some basics:

- Bristle brush
- Grooming glove
- Metal comb
- Rubber mat
- Dog shampoo
- Spray hose attachment
- Towels
- Ear cleaner
- Cotton balls
- Nail clippers
- Dental-care products

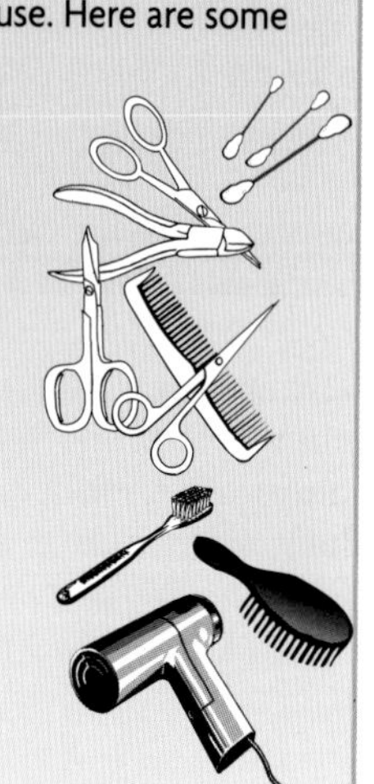

useful to give the dog a wipe-down with a damp cloth, but never leave a dog damp in cold weather or in a draft.

Dogs do not need to be bathed as often as humans, but bathing as needed is important for healthy skin and a clean, shiny coat. Again, like most anything, if you accustom your pup to being bathed as a puppy, it will be second nature by the time he grows up. You want your dog to be at ease in the bath or else it could end up a wet, soapy, messy ordeal for both of you!

Brush your Toy Manchester thoroughly before wetting his coat. This will get rid of any dead hair and debris, which are harder to remove when the coat is wet.

Make certain that your dog has a good non-slip surface to stand on. Begin by wetting the dog's coat. A shower or hose attachment is necessary for thoroughly wetting and rinsing the coat. Check the water temperature to make sure that it is neither too hot nor too cold.

Next, apply shampoo to the dog's coat and work it into a good lather. You should purchase a shampoo that is made for dogs. Do not use a product made for human hair. Wash the head last; you do not want shampoo to drip into the dog's eyes while you are washing the rest of his body. Work the shampoo all the way down to the skin. You can use this opportunity to check the skin for any bumps, bites or other abnormalities. Do not neglect any area of the body—get all of the hard-to-reach places.

Once the dog has been thoroughly shampooed, he requires an equally thorough rinsing. Shampoo left in the coat can be irritating to the skin. Protect his eyes from the shampoo by shielding them with your hand and directing the flow of water in the

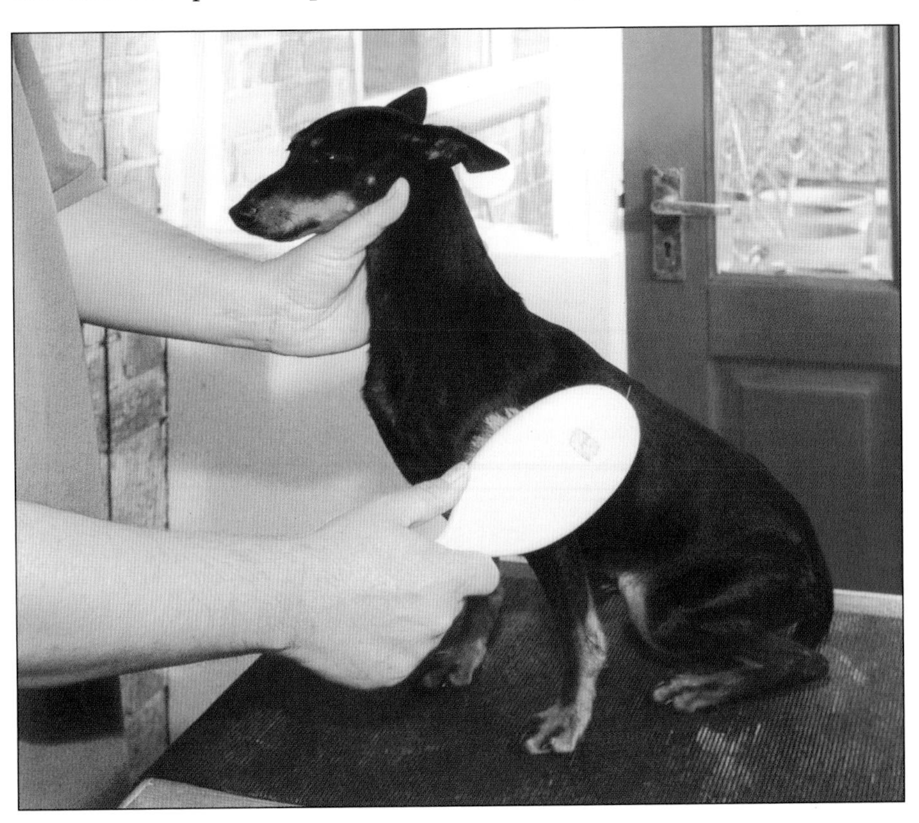

A soft-bristle brush can be used to remove the dead hairs from your Toy Manchester's coat.

With the Toy Manchester's black nails, it's best to clip only a small bit of the nail at a time or to use a file where the quick is not visible.

In light-colored nails, clipping is much simpler because you can see the vein (or quick) that grows inside the nail casing.

opposite direction. You should also avoid getting water in the ear canal. Be prepared for your dog to shake out his coat—you might want to stand back, but make sure you have a hold on the dog to keep him from running through the house and have a towel ready.

Ear Care

It is always necessary to keep a dog's ears clean, and this is especially important in the case of a Toy Manchester, which has such prominent, if small, ears. Ears should be kept clean using a special cleaner, but take care not to delve into the ear canal as this might cause injury.

Nails

Never forget that toenails should be kept short. How frequently the

PEDICURE TIP

A dog that spends a lot of time outside on a hard surface, such as cement or pavement, will have his nails naturally worn down and may not need to have them trimmed as often, except maybe in the colder months when he is not outside as much. Regardless, it is best to get your dog accustomed to the nail-trimming procedure at an early age so that he is used to it. Some dogs are especially sensitive about having their feet touched, but if a dog has experienced it since puppyhood, it should not bother him.

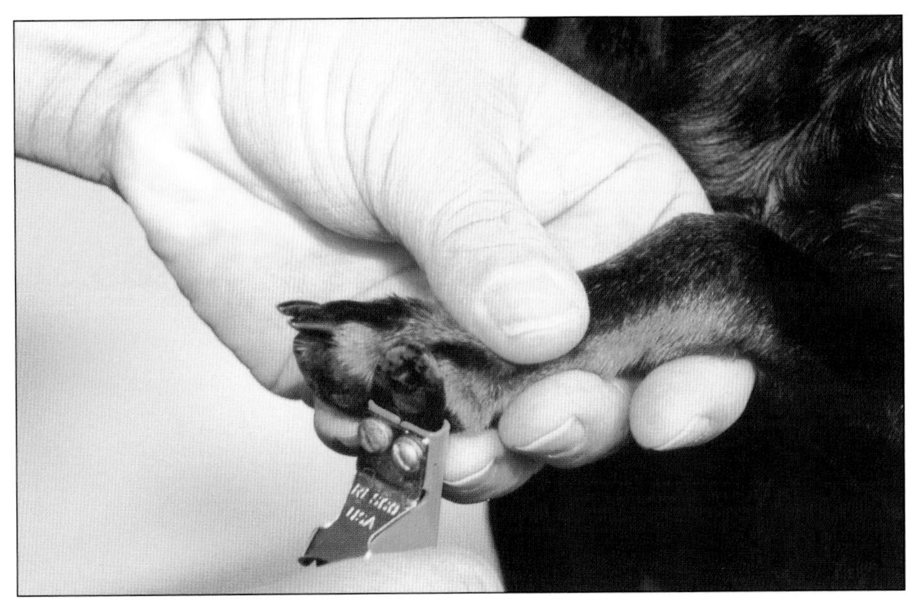

Your local pet shop has special clippers for cutting your dog's nails. The guillotine-type (pictured) are ideal for the Toy Manchester.

nails will need to be clipped will depend on how much the dog walks on hard surfaces, but they should be checked on a weekly basis. Canine nail clippers can easily be obtained from pet shops, and many owners find those of the guillotine design easier to use. A nail file can also be used to give a good finish to the nails. However, it is important to introduce a Toy Manchester to routine nail care from an early age, for many can be very awkward about this.

TEETH

Teeth should always be kept as free from tartar as possible. There are now several canine tooth-cleaning agents available, including the basics, like a small toothbrush and canine toothpaste.

DEADLY DECAY

Did you know that periodontal disease (a condition of the bone and gums surrounding a tooth) can be fatal? Having your dog's teeth and mouth checked yearly, along with regular tooth-brushing at home, can prevent periodontal disease.

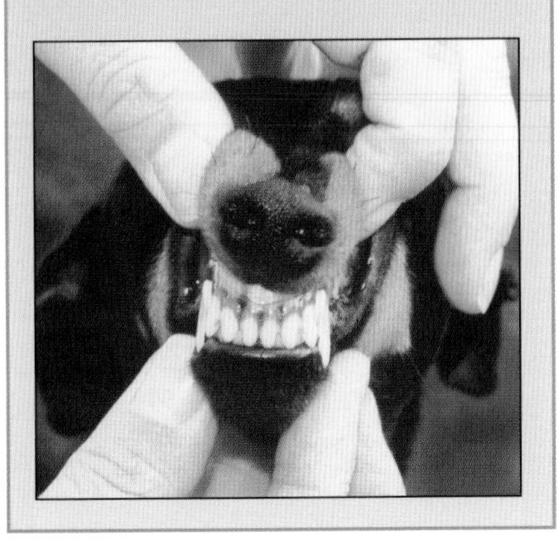

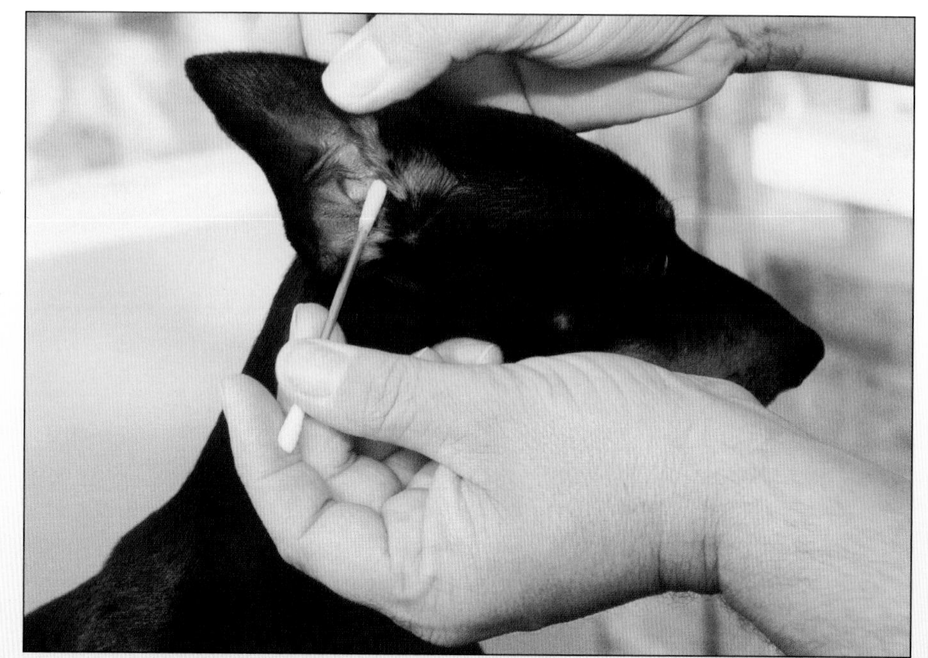

Be careful when cleaning your dog's ears. Use a soft cloth or cotton swab to clean the outer ear gently. *Never* probe into the ear canal.

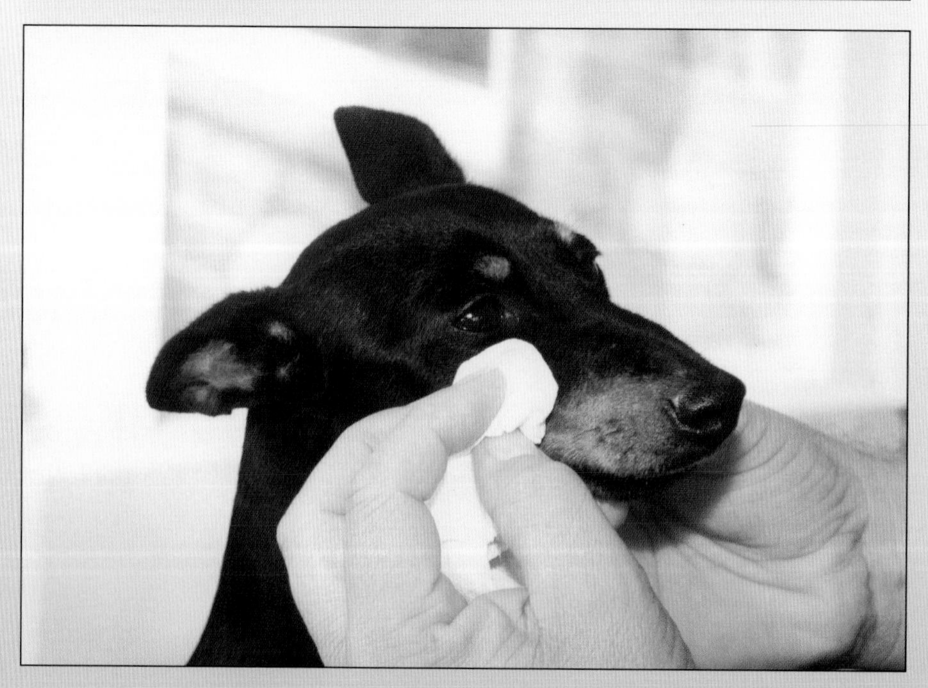

The eye area can be cleansed by gently using a soft damp cloth.

TRAVELING WITH YOUR DOG

Car Travel

You should accustom your Toy Manchester Terrier to riding in a car at an early age. You may or may not take him in the car often, but at the very least he will need to go to the vet and you do not want these trips to be traumatic for the dog or troublesome for you. The safest way for a dog to ride in the car is in his crate. If he uses a crate in the house, you can use the same crate for travel.

Put the pup in the crate and see how he reacts. If he seems uneasy, you can have a passenger hold him on his lap while you drive. Another option is a specially made safety harness for dogs, which straps the dog in much like a seat belt. Do not let the dog roam loose in the vehicle—this is very dangerous! If you should stop short, your dog can be thrown and injured. If the dog starts climbing on you and pestering you while you are driving, you will not be able to concentrate on the road. It is an unsafe situation for everyone—human and canine.

For long trips, bring along some water for the dog and be prepared to stop to let him relieve himself. Take with you whatever you need to clean up after him, including some paper

COLLAR REQUIRED

If your dog gets lost, he is not able to ask for directions home. Identification tags fastened to the collar give important information—the dog's name, the owner's name, the owner's address and a telephone number where the owner can be reached. This makes it easy for whomever finds the dog to contact the owner and arrange to have the dog returned. An added advantage is that a person will be more likely to approach a lost dog who has ID tags on his collar; it tells the person that this is somebody's pet rather than a stray. This is the easiest and fastest method of identification, provided that the tags stay on the collar and the collar stays on the dog.

Show-dog owners get used to traveling with all of the necessities—crate, toys, grooming supplies, etc.

Standard Manchester Terriers are easy to transport by car but their larger size prohibits them from carry-on status on an airplane.

towels and perhaps some old rags for use should he have a potty accident in the car or suffer from motion sickness.

TRAVEL TIP

Never leave your dog alone in the car. In hot weather, your dog can die from the high temperature inside a closed vehicle; even a car parked in the shade can heat up very quickly. Leaving the window open is dangerous as well since the dog can hurt himself trying to get out.

Air Travel

Contact your chosen airline before proceeding with travel plans that include your Toy Manchester. The dog will be required to travel in a fiberglass crate and you should always check in advance with the airline regarding specific requirements for the crate's size, type and labeling, as well as needed health certificates and travel restrictions.

To help put the dog at ease, give him one of his favorite toys in the crate. Do not feed the dog for several hours prior to checking in so that you minimize his need to relieve himself. Some airlines require you to document when the dog was last fed. In any case a light meal is best. For long trips, you will have to attach food and water bowls to the dog's crate so that airline employees can tend to him between legs of the trip.

Make sure your dog is properly identified and that your contact information appears on his ID tags and on his crate. Many airlines permit small dogs to travel with their owners in the cabin, and the Toy Manchester is certainly a nice pocket-sized dog who can travel comfortably in his crate tucked under his master's seat. Discuss this option with your chosen airline, and if necessary switch airlines until you find one that lets your Toy Manchester "fly the friendly skies" alongside you.

Vacations and Boarding

So you want to take a family trip—and you want to include *all* members of the family. You would probably make arrangements for accommodations ahead of time anyway, but this is especially important when traveling with a dog. You do not want to make an overnight stop at the only place around for miles and find out that they do not allow dogs. Also, you do not want to reserve a place for your family without confirming that you are traveling with a dog because, if it is against the hotel's policy, you may end up without a place to stay.

Alternatively, if you are trav-

IDENTIFICATION OPTIONS

As puppies become more and more expensive, especially those puppies of high quality for showing and/or breeding, they have a greater chance of being stolen. The usual collar dog tag is, of course, easily removed. But there are two more permanent techniques that have become widely used for identifying dogs.

The puppy microchip implantation involves the injection of a small microchip, about the size of a corn kernel, under the skin of the dog. If your dog shows up at a clinic or shelter, or is offered for resale under less-than-savory circumstances, he can be positively identified by the microchip. The microchip is scanned, and a registry quickly identifies you as the owner.

Tattooing is done on various parts of the dog, from his belly to his ears. The number tattooed can be your telephone number, the dog's registration number or any other number that you can easily memorize. When professional dog thieves see a tattooed dog, they usually lose interest. For the safety of our dogs, no laboratory facility or dog broker will accept a tattooed dog as stock.

Discuss microchipping and tattooing with your vet and breeder. Some vets perform these services on their own premises for a reasonable fee. To ensure that the dog's ID is effective, be certain that the dog is then properly registered with a legitimate national database.

eling and choose not to bring your Toy Manchester, you will have to make arrangements for him while you are away. Some options are to take him to a friend's house to stay while you are gone, to have a familiar neighbor stop by often or stay at your house or to bring your dog to a reputable boarding kennel. If you choose to board him at a kennel, you should visit in advance to see the facilities provided, how clean they are and where the dogs are kept. Talk to some of the employees and see how they treat the dogs—do they spend time with the dogs, play with them, exercise them, etc.? Also find out the kennel's policy on vaccinations and what they require. This is for all of the dogs' safety, since when dogs are kept together, there is a greater risk of diseases being passed from dog to dog.

A sturdy everyday collar with your dog's ID tags attached is required for proper identification.

Find a boarding kennel that considers the special needs of small dogs like the Toy Manchester Terrier. Your vet may be an option, as some vets offer boarding facilities.

CONSIDERING BOARDING?

Will your dog be exercised at least twice a day? How often during the day will the staff keep him company? Does the kennel provide a clean and secure environment? These are some of the questions you should consider when choosing a suitable boarding kennel.

Likewise, if the staff asks you a lot of questions, this is a good sign. They need to know your dog's personality and temperament, health record, special requirements and what commands he has learned. Above all, follow your instincts. If you have a bad feeling about a kennel, even if a friend has recommended it, don't put your dog in their care.

IDENTIFICATION

Your Toy Manchester is your valued companion and friend. That is why you always keep a close eye on him and you have made sure that he cannot escape from the yard or wriggle out of his collar and run away from you. However, accidents can happen and there may come a time when your dog unexpectedly gets separated from you. If this unfortunate event should occur, the first thing on your mind will be finding him. Proper identification, including an ID tag, and possibly a tattoo and/or a microchip, will increase the chances of his being returned to you quickly.

TRAINING YOUR

TOY MANCHESTER TERRIER

Living with an untrained dog is a lot like owning a piano that you do not know how to play—it is a nice object to look at, but it does not do much more than that to bring you pleasure. Now try taking piano lessons, and suddenly the piano comes alive and brings forth magical sounds and rhythms that set your heart singing and your body swaying.

The same is true with your Toy Manchester Terrier. Any dog is a big responsibility and, if not trained sensibly, may develop unacceptable behavior that annoys you or could even cause family friction.

To train your Toy Manchester Terrier, you may like to enroll in an obedience class. Teach him good manners as you learn how and why he behaves the way he does. Find out how to communicate with your dog and how to recognize and understand his communications with you. Suddenly the dog takes on a new role in your life—he is clever, interesting, well-behaved and fun to be with. He demonstrates his bond of devotion to you daily. In other words, your Toy Manchester does wonders for your ego because he constantly reminds you that you are not only his leader, you are his hero!

Those involved with teaching

REAP THE REWARDS

If you start with a normal, healthy dog and give him time, patience and some carefully executed lessons, you will reap the rewards of that training for the life of the dog. And what a life it will be! The two of you will find immeasurable pleasure in the companionship you have built together with love, respect and understanding.

> **FAMILY TIES**
> If you have other pets in the home and/or interact often with the pets of friends and other family members, your pup will respond to those pets in much the same manner as you do. It is only when you show fear of or resentment toward another animal that he will act fearful or unfriendly.

dog obedience and counseling owners about their dogs' behavior have discovered some interesting facts about dog ownership. For example, training dogs when they are puppies results in the highest rate of success in developing well-mannered and well-adjusted adult dogs. Training an older dog, from six months to six years of age, can produce almost equal results, providing that the owner accepts the dog's slower rate of learning capability and is willing to work patiently to help the dog succeed at developing to his fullest potential. Unfortunately, many owners of untrained adult dogs lack the patience factor, so they do not persist until their dogs are successful at learning particular behaviors.

Training a puppy aged 10 to 16 weeks (20 weeks at the most) is like working with a dry sponge in a pool of water. The pup soaks up whatever you show him and constantly looks for more things to do and learn. At this early age, his body is not yet producing hormones, and therein lies the reason for such a high rate of success. Without hormones, he is focused on his owners and not particularly interested in investigating other places, dogs, people, etc. You are his leader: his provider of food, water, shelter and security. He latches onto you and wants to stay close. He will usually follow you from room to room, will not let you out of his sight when you are outdoors with him and will respond in like manner to the people and animals you encounter. If you greet a friend warmly, he will be happy to greet the person as well. If, however, you are hesitant or anxious about the approach of a stranger, he will respond accordingly.

Once the puppy begins to produce hormones, his natural

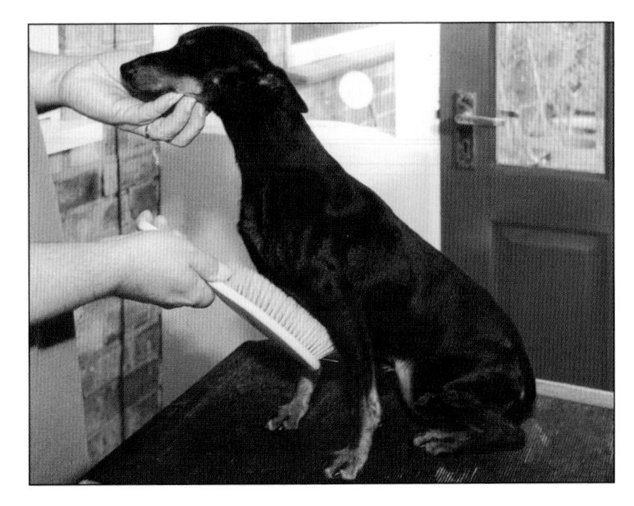

Time spent grooming, training and caring for your dog result in a well-behaved companion animal that is a pleasure to be around.

SAFETY FIRST

While it may seem that the most important things to your dog are eating, sleeping and chewing the upholstery on your furniture, his first concern is actually safety. The domesticated dogs we keep as companions have the same pack instinct as their ancestors who ran free thousands of years ago. Because of this pack instinct, your dog wants to know that he and his pack are not in danger of being harmed, and that his pack has a strong, capable leader. You must establish yourself as the leader early on in your relationship. That way your dog will trust that you will take care of him and the pack, and he will accept your commands without question.

curiosity emerges and he begins to investigate the world around him. It is at this time when you may notice that the untrained dog begins to wander away from you and even ignore your commands to stay close. When this behavior becomes a problem, the owner has two choices: get rid of the dog or train him. It is

Your Toy Manchester's bowl should kept in a low-traffic place so that he can eat without distraction or interruption.

strongly urged that you choose the latter option.

There usually will be classes within a reasonable distance from your home, but you can also do a lot to train your dog yourself. Sometimes there are classes available but the tuition is too costly. Whatever the circumstances, the solution to training your dog without formal obedience lessons lies within the pages of this book.

FEAR AGGRESSION

Pups who are subjected to physical abuse during training commonly end up with behavioral problems as adults. One common result of abuse is fear aggression, in which a dog will lash out, bare his teeth, snarl and finally bite someone by whom he feels threatened. For example, your daughter may be playing with the dog one afternoon. As they play hide-and-seek, she backs the dog into a corner and, as she attempts to tease him playfully, he bites her hand. Examine the cause of this behavior. Did your daughter ever hit the dog? Did someone who resembles your daughter hit or scream at the dog?

Fortunately, fear aggression is relatively easy to correct. Have your daughter engage in only positive activities with the dog, such as feeding, petting and walking. She should not give any corrections or negative feedback. If the dog still growls or cowers away from her, allow someone else to accompany them. After approximately one week, the dog should feel that he can rely on her for many positive things, and he will also be prevented from reacting fearfully towards anyone who might resemble her.

If you intend to show your Toy Manchester puppy, begin setting him up on a grooming table right away. In well-trained show dogs, standing proud on a table seems second nature.

CALM DOWN

Dogs will do anything for your attention. If you reward the dog when he is calm and attentive, you will develop a well-mannered dog. If, on the other hand, you greet your dog excitedly and encourage him to wrestle with you, the dog will greet you the same way and you will have a hyperactive dog on your hands.

This chapter is devoted to helping you train your Toy Manchester at home. If the recommended procedures are followed faithfully, you may expect positive results that will prove rewarding both to you and your dog.

Whether your new charge is a puppy or a mature adult, the methods of teaching and the techniques we use in training basic behaviors are the same. After all, no dog, whether puppy or adult, likes harsh or inhumane methods. All creatures, however, respond favorably to gentle motivational methods and sincere praise and encouragement. Now let us get started.

HOUSE-TRAINING

You can train a puppy to relieve himself wherever you choose, but this must be somewhere suitable. You should bear in mind from the outset that when your puppy is old enough to go out in public places, any canine deposits must be removed at once. You will always have to carry with you a small plastic bag or "poop-scoop."

Outdoor training includes such surfaces as grass, soil and cement. Indoor training usually means training your dog to newspaper. When deciding on the surface and location that you will want your Toy Manchester to use, be sure it is going to be

> **HONOR AND OBEY**
> Dogs are the most honorable animals in existence. They consider another species (humans) as their own. They interface with you. You are their leader. Puppies perceive children to be on their level; their actions around small children are different from their behavior around their adult masters.

permanent. Training your dog to grass and then changing your mind two months later is extremely difficult for both dog and owner.

Next, choose the command you will use each and every time you want your puppy to relieve himself. "Hurry up" and "Potty" are examples of commands commonly used by dog owners. Get in the habit of giving the puppy your chosen relief command before you take him out. That way, when he becomes an adult, you will be able to determine if he wants to go out when you ask him. A confirmation will be signs of interest, such as wagging his tail, watching you intently, going to the door, etc.

PUPPY'S NEEDS

Your puppy needs to relieve himself after play periods, after each meal, after he has been sleeping and at any time he indicates that he is looking for a place to urinate or defecate. The urinary and intestinal tract muscles of very young puppies are not fully developed. Therefore, like human babies, puppies need to relieve themselves frequently.

Take your puppy out often—every hour for a ten-week-old, for example, and always immediately after sleeping and eating. The older the puppy, the less often he will need to relieve himself. Finally, as a mature healthy adult, he will require only three to five relief trips per day.

HOUSING

Since the types of housing and control you provide for your puppy have a direct relationship on the success of house-training,

Clean habits must be instilled in the very young puppy. Dogs do not like to soil their crates, dog beds or other favorite areas, so training him to relieve himself outside his quarters should begin early.

CANINE DEVELOPMENT SCHEDULE

It is important to understand how and at what age a puppy develops into adulthood. If you are a puppy owner, consult the following Canine Development Schedule to determine the stage of development your puppy is currently experiencing. This knowledge will help you as you work with the puppy in the weeks and months ahead.

Period	Age	Characteristics
First to Third	Birth to Seven Weeks	Puppy needs food, sleep and warmth, and responds to simple and gentle touching. Needs mother for security and disciplining. Needs littermates for learning and interacting with other dogs. Pup learns to function within a pack and learns pack order of dominance. Begin socializing pup with adults and children for short periods. Pup begins to become aware of his environment.
Fourth	Eight to Twelve Weeks	Brain is fully developed. Needs socializing with outside world. Remove from mother and littermates. Needs to change from canine pack to human pack. Human dominance necessary. Fear period occurs between 8 and 12 weeks. Avoid fright and pain.
Fifth	Thirteen to Sixteen Weeks	Training and formal obedience should begin. Less association with other dogs, more with people, places, situations. Period will pass easily if you remember this is pup's change-to-adolescence time. Be firm and fair. Flight instinct prominent. Permissiveness and over-disciplining can do permanent damage. Praise for good behavior.
Juvenile	Four to Eight Months	Another fear period about 7 to 8 months of age. It passes quickly, but be cautious of fright and pain. Sexual maturity reached. Dominant traits established. Dog should understand sit, down, come and stay by now.

Note: These are approximate time frames. Allow for individual differences in puppies.

House-training a puppy to newspaper is sometimes done with small dogs like the Toy Manchester. Breeders frequently begin paper-training before the litter leaves the premises.

we consider the various aspects of both before we begin training. Taking a new puppy home and turning him loose in your house can be compared to turning a child loose in a sports arena and telling the child that the place is all his! The sheer enormity of the place would be too much for him to handle.

PAPER CAPER

Never line your pup's sleeping area with newspaper. Puppy litters are usually raised on newspaper and, once in your home, the puppy will immediately associate newspaper with voiding. Never put newspaper on any floor while house-training, as this will only confuse the puppy. If you are paper-training him, use paper in his designated relief area only. Finally, restrict water intake after evening meals. Offer a few licks at a time—never let a young puppy (or an adult) gulp water after meals.

Instead, offer the puppy clearly defined areas where he can play, sleep, eat and live. A room of the house where the family gathers is the most obvious choice. Puppies are social animals and need to feel a part of the pack right from the start. Hearing your voice, watching you while you are doing things and smelling you nearby are all positive reinforcers that he is now a member of your pack. Usually a family room, the kitchen or a nearby adjoining breakfast area is ideal for providing safety and security for both puppy and owner.

Within that room, there should be a smaller area that the puppy can call his own. An alcove, a wire or fiberglass dog crate or a partitioned (not boarded!) corner from which he can view the activities of his new family will be fine. The size of the area or crate is the key factor here. The area must be large enough for the puppy to lie down and stretch out as well as stand up without rubbing his head on the top, yet small enough so that he cannot relieve himself at one end and sleep at the other without coming into contact with his droppings. Dogs are, by nature, clean animals and will not remain close to their relief areas unless forced to do

HOW MANY TIMES A DAY?

AGE	RELIEF TRIPS
To 14 weeks	10
14–22 weeks	8
22–32 weeks	6
Adulthood (dog stops growing)	4

These are estimates, of course, but they are a guide to the *minimum* number of opportunities a dog should have each day to relieve himself.

Always clean up after your dog, whether you are in a public place or in your own yard. Your local pet shop has gadgets to help in the cleanup task.

so. In those cases, they then become dirty dogs and usually remain that way for life.

The designated area should contain clean bedding and a toy. Water must always be available for your dog, but avoid putting food and water in his crate until he is reliably house-trained.

TAKE THE LEAD

Do not carry your dog to his relief area. Lead him there on a leash or, better yet, encourage him to follow you to the spot. If you start carrying him to his spot, you might end up doing this routine forever and your dog will have the satisfaction of having trained *you*.

CONTROL

By control, we mean helping the puppy to create a lifestyle pattern that will be compatible to that of his human pack (you). Just as we guide little children to learn our way of life, we must show the puppy when it is time to play, eat, sleep, exercise and even entertain himself.

Your puppy should always sleep in his crate. He should also learn that, during times of household confusion and excessive human activity such as at breakfast when family members are preparing for the day, he can play by himself in relative safety and comfort in his designated area. Each time you leave the puppy alone, he should understand exactly where he is to stay. Puppies are chewers. They cannot tell the difference between lamp cords, television wires, shoes, table legs, etc. Chewing into a television wire, for example, can be fatal to the puppy, while a shorted wire can start a fire in the house.

If the puppy chews on the

arm of the chair when he is alone, you will probably discipline him angrily when you get home. Thus, he makes the association that your coming home means he is going to be punished. (He will not remember chewing the chair and is incapable of making the association of the discipline with his naughty deed.) Crating the pup avoids his engaging in dangerous and/or destructive behaviors when you're not there to supervise.

Other times of excitement, such as holidays, family parties, etc., can be fun for the puppy providing he can view the activi-

THE SUCCESS METHOD

Success that comes by luck is usually short-lived. Success that comes by well-thought-out proven methods is often more easily achieved and permanent. This is the Success Method. It is designed to give you, the puppy owner, a simple yet proven way to help your puppy develop clean living habits and a feeling of security in his new environment.

6 Steps to Successful Crate Training

1 Tell the puppy "Crate time!" and place him in the crate with a small treat (a piece of cheese or half of a biscuit). Let him stay in the crate for five minutes while you are in the same room. Then release him and praise lavishly. Never release him when he is fussing. Wait until he is quiet before you let him out.

2 Repeat Step 1 several times a day.

3 The next day, place the puppy in the crate as before. Let him stay there for ten minutes. Do this several times.

4 Continue building time in five-minute increments until the puppy stays in his crate for 30 minutes with you in the room. Always take him to his relief area after prolonged periods in his crate.

5 Now go back to Step 1 and let the puppy stay in his crate for five minutes, this time while you are out of the room.

6 Once again, build crate time in five-minute increments with you out of the room. When the puppy will stay willingly in his crate (he may even fall asleep!) for 30 minutes with you out of the room, he will be ready to stay in it for several hours at a time.

ties from the security of his designated area. He is not underfoot and he is not being fed all sorts of tidbits that will probably cause him stomach distress, yet he still feels a part of the fun.

SCHEDULE

Your puppy should be taken to his relief area each time he is released from his designated area, after meals, after play sessions and when he first awakens in the morning (at age ten weeks, this can mean 5 a.m.!). The puppy will indicate that he's ready "to go" by circling or sniffing busily—do not misinterpret these signs. For a puppy around ten weeks of age, a routine of taking him out every hour is necessary. As the puppy grows, he will be able to wait for longer periods of time.

Keep trips to his relief area short. Stay no more than five or six minutes and then return to the house. If he goes during that time, praise him lavishly and take him indoors immediately. If he does not, but he has an accident when you go back indoors, pick him up immediately, say "No! No!" and return to his relief area. Wait a few minutes, then return to the house again. Never hit a puppy or put his face in urine or excrement when he has had an accident!

Once indoors, put the puppy in his crate until you have had time to clean up his accident. Then release him to the family area and watch him more closely than before. Chances are, his accident was a result of your not picking up his signal or waiting

HOUSE-TRAINING TIP

Most of all, be consistent. Always take your dog to the same location, always use the same command and always have the dog on lead when he is in his relief area, unless a fenced-in yard is available.

By following the Success Method, your puppy will be completely housebroken by the time his muscle and brain development reach maturity. Keep in mind that small breeds usually mature faster than large breeds, but all puppies should be trained by six months of age.

Most dogs naturally respond to grass for their relief areas. If you intend for your dog to use the great outdoors as his bathroom, lead him to a grassy patch every time you release him to go out.

too long before offering him the opportunity to relieve himself. Never hold a grudge against the puppy for accidents.

Let the puppy learn that going outdoors means it is time to relieve himself, not play. Once trained, he will be able to play indoors and out and still differentiate between the times for play versus the times for relief.

Help him develop regular hours for naps, being alone, playing by himself and just resting, all in his crate. Encourage him to entertain himself while you are busy with your activities. Let him learn that having you near is comforting, but it is not your main purpose in life to provide him with undivided attention.

Each time you put your puppy in his own area, use the same command, whatever suits best. Soon he will run to his crate or special area when he hears you say those words. Crate training provides safety for you, the puppy and the home. It also provides the puppy with a feeling of security, and that helps the puppy achieve self-confidence and clean habits.

Remember that one of the primary ingredients in house-training your puppy is control. Regardless of your lifestyle, there will always be occasions when you will need to have a place where your dog can stay and be happy and safe. Crate training is the answer for now and in the future.

In conclusion, a few key elements are really all you need for a successful house-training method—consistency, frequency, praise, control and supervision. By following these procedures

THE CLEAN LIFE

By providing sleeping and resting quarters that fit the dog, and offering frequent opportunities to relieve himself outside his quarters, the puppy quickly learns that the outdoors (or the newspaper if you are training him to paper) is the place to go when he needs to urinate or defecate. It also reinforces his innate desire to keep his sleeping quarters clean. This, in turn, helps develop the muscle control that will eventually produce a dog with clean living habits.

PRACTICE MAKES PERFECT!

- Have training lessons with your dog every day in several short segments—three to five times a day for a few minutes at a time is ideal.
- Do not have long practice sessions. The dog will become easily bored.
- Never practice when you are tired, ill, worried or in an otherwise negative mood. This will transmit to the dog and may have an adverse effect on his performance.

Think fun, short and above all *positive*! End each session on a high note, rather than a failed exercise, and make sure to give a lot of praise. Enjoy the training and help your dog enjoy it, too.

with a normal, healthy puppy, you and the puppy will soon be past the stage of "accidents" and ready to move on to a full and rewarding life together.

ROLES OF DISCIPLINE, REWARD AND PUNISHMENT

Discipline, training one to act in accordance with rules, brings order to life. It is as simple as that. Without discipline, particularly in a group society, chaos reigns supreme and the group will eventually perish. Humans and canines are social animals and need some form of discipline in order to function effectively. They must procure food, reproduce to keep the species going and protect their home base and their young. If there were no discipline in the lives of social animals, they would eventually die from starvation and/or predation by other stronger animals. In the case of domestic canines, dogs need discipline in their lives in order to understand how their pack (you and other family members) functions and how they must act in order to survive.

A large humane society in a highly populated area recently surveyed dog owners regarding their satisfaction with their relationships with their dogs. People who had trained their dogs were 75% more satisfied with their pets than those who had never trained their dogs.

Dr. Edward Thorndike, a noted psychologist, established *Thorndike's Theory of Learning,*

Toy Manchester Terriers are sensitive dogs, and, like all other dogs, respond to fairness and kindness. Never abuse or forcefully scold your TMT.

which states that a behavior that results in a pleasant event tends to be repeated. A behavior that results in an unpleasant event tends not to be repeated. It is this theory on which training methods are based today. For example, if you manipulate a dog to perform a specific behavior and reward him for doing it, he is likely to do it again because he enjoyed the end result.

EASY DOES IT

Gently laying your hand over the top of the dog's neck right behind the ears acts as a dominant signal. Adding a soothing, soft voice with the word "easy" can calm an overly excited dog and help him resume a normal attitude.

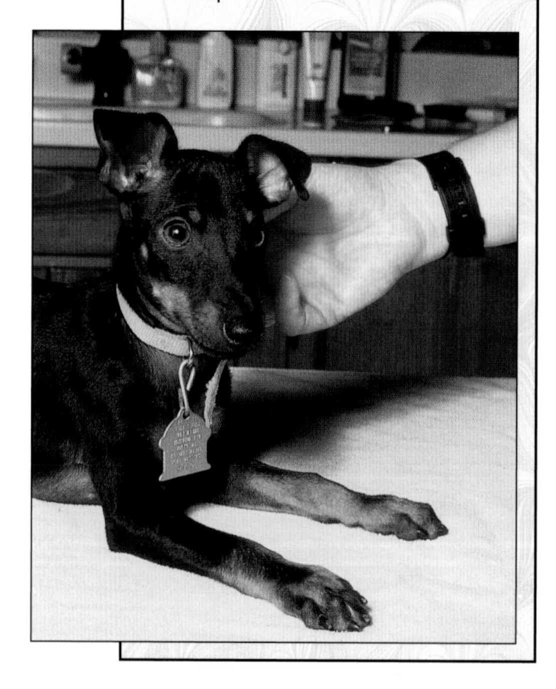

Occasionally, punishment, a penalty inflicted for an offense, is necessary. The best type of punishment often comes from an outside source. For example, a child is told not to touch the stove because he may get burned. He disobeys and touches the stove. In doing so, he receives a burn. From that time on, he respects the heat of the stove and avoids contact with it. Therefore, a behavior that results in an unpleasant event tends not to be repeated.

A good example of a dog learning the hard way is the dog who chases the house cat. He is told many times to leave the cat alone, yet he persists in teasing the cat. Then, one day he begins chasing the cat but the cat turns and swipes a claw across the dog's face, leaving him with a painful gash on his nose. The final result is that the dog stops chasing the cat.

TRAINING EQUIPMENT

COLLAR AND LEASH

For a Toy Manchester Terrier, the collar and leash that you use for training must be one with which you are easily able to work, not too heavy for the dog and perfectly safe.

TREATS

Have a bag of treats on hand. Something nutritious and easy to

THE GOLDEN RULE

The golden rule of dog training is simple. For each "question" (command), there is only one correct answer (reaction). One command = one reaction. Keep practicing the command until the dog reacts correctly without hesitating. Be repetitive but not monotonous. Dogs get bored just as people do!

swallow works best. Use a soft treat, a chunk of cheese or a piece of cooked chicken rather than a dry biscuit. By the time the dog has finished chewing a dry treat, he will forget why he is being rewarded in the first place! Using food rewards will not teach a dog to beg at the table—the only way to teach a dog to beg at the table is to give him food from the table. In training, rewarding the dog with a food treat will help him associate praise and the treats with learning new behaviors that obviously please his owner.

TRAINING BEGINS: ASK THE DOG A QUESTION

In order to teach your dog anything, you must first get his attention. After all, he cannot learn anything if he is looking away from you with his mind on something else.

To get his attention, ask him "School?" and immediately walk over to him and give him a treat as you tell him "Good dog." Wait a minute or two and repeat the routine, this time with a treat in your hand as you approach within a foot of the dog. Do not go directly to him, but stop about a foot short of him and hold out the treat as you ask "School?" He will see you approaching with a treat in your hand and most likely begin walking toward you. As you meet, give him the treat and praise again.

The third time, ask the question, have a treat in your hand and walk only a short distance toward the dog so that he must walk almost all the way to you. As he reaches you, give him the treat and praise again.

By this time, the dog will probably be getting the idea that if he pays attention to you, especially when you ask that question, it will pay off in treats and enjoyable activities for him. In other words, he learns that "school" means doing great things with you that are fun and result in positive attention for him.

Remember that the dog does not understand your verbal language; he only recognizes sounds. Your question translates to a series of sounds for him, and those sounds become the signal to go to you and pay attention; if he does, he will get to interact with you plus receive treats and praise.

THE BASIC COMMANDS

Teaching Sit

Now that you have the dog's attention, attach his lead and hold it in your left hand and a food treat in your right. Place your food hand at the dog's nose and let him lick the treat but not take it from you. Say "Sit" and slowly raise your food hand from in front of the dog's nose up over his head so that he is looking at the ceiling. As he bends his head upward, he will have to bend his knees to maintain his balance. As he bends

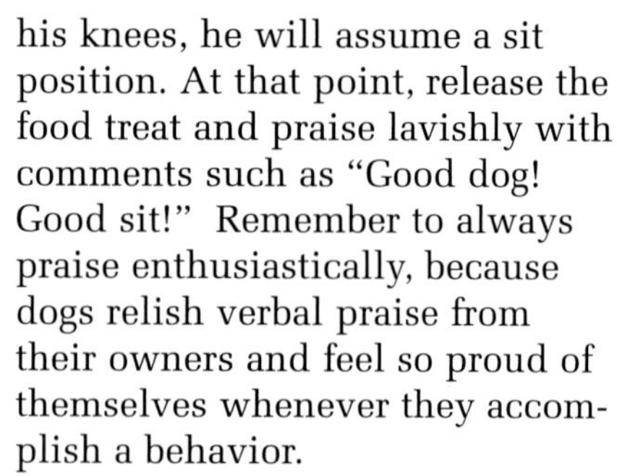

his knees, he will assume a sit position. At that point, release the food treat and praise lavishly with comments such as "Good dog! Good sit!" Remember to always praise enthusiastically, because dogs relish verbal praise from their owners and feel so proud of themselves whenever they accomplish a behavior.

You will not use food forever in getting the dog to obey your commands. Food is only used to teach new behaviors, and once the dog knows what you want when you give a specific command, you will wean him off the food treats but still maintain the verbal praise. After all, you will always have your voice with you, and there will be many times when you have no food rewards but expect the dog to obey.

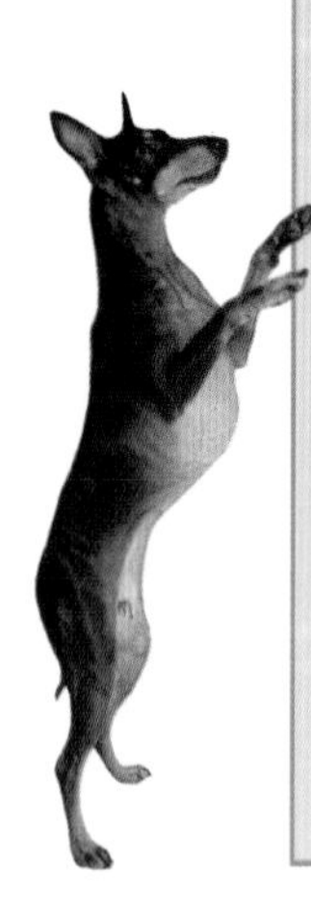

THE STUDENT'S STRESS TEST

During training sessions, you must be able to recognize signs of stress in your dog such as:

- tucking his tail between his legs
- lowering his head
- shivering or trembling
- standing completely still or running away
- panting and/or salivating
- avoiding eye contact
- flattening his ears back
- urinating submissively
- rolling over and lifting a leg
- grinning or baring teeth
- aggression when restrained

If your four-legged student displays these signs, he may just be nervous or intimidated. The training session may have been too lengthy, with not enough praise and affirmation. Stop for the day and try again tomorrow.

Teaching Down

Teaching the down exercise is easy when you understand how the dog perceives the down position, and it is very difficult when you do not. Dogs perceive the down position as a submissive one; therefore, teaching the down exercise using a forceful method can sometimes make the dog develop such a fear of the down that he either runs away when you say "Down" or he attempts to snap at the person who tries to force him down.

Have the dog sit close alongside your left leg, facing in the same direction as you are. Hold the lead in your left hand and a food treat in your right. Now place your left hand lightly on the top of the dog's shoulders where they meet above the spinal cord. Do not push down on the dog's shoulders; simply rest your left hand there so you can guide the dog to lie down close to your left leg rather than to swing away from your side when he drops.

Now place the food hand at the dog's nose, say "Down" very softly (almost a whisper) and slowly lower the food hand to the dog's front feet. When the food hand reaches the floor, begin moving it forward along the floor in front of the dog. Keep talking softly to the dog, saying things like, "Do you want this treat? You can do this, good dog." Your reassuring tone of voice will help calm the dog as he tries to follow the food hand in order to get the treat.

When the dog's elbows touch the floor, release the food and praise softly. Try to get the dog to maintain that down position for several seconds before you let him sit up again. The goal here is to get the dog to settle down and not feel threatened in the down position.

DOUBLE JEOPARDY

A dog in jeopardy never lies down. He stays alert on his feet because instinct tells him that he may have to run away or fight for his survival. Therefore, if a dog feels threatened or anxious, he will not lie down. Consequently, it is important to keep the dog calm and relaxed as he learns the down exercise.

Teaching Stay

It is easy to teach the dog to stay in either a sit or a down position. Again, we use food and praise during the teaching process as we help the dog to understand exactly what it is that we are expecting him to do.

To teach the sit/stay, start with the dog sitting on your left side as before and hold the lead in your left hand. Have a food treat in your right hand and place your food hand at the dog's nose. Say "Stay" and step out on your right foot to stand directly in front of the dog, toe to toe, as he licks and nibbles the treat. Be sure to keep his head facing upward to maintain the sit position. Count to five and then swing around to

CONSISTENCY PAYS OFF

Dogs need consistency in their feeding schedule, exercise and relief visits, and in the verbal commands you use. If you use "Stay" on Monday and "Stay here, please" on Tuesday, you will confuse your dog. Don't demand perfect behavior during training sessions and then let him have the run of the house the rest of the day. Above all, lavish praise on your pet consistently every time he does something right. The more he feels he is pleasing you, the more willing he will be to learn.

stand next to the dog again with him on your left. As soon as you get back to the original position, release the food and praise lavishly.

To teach the down/stay, do the down as previously described. As soon as the dog lies down, say "Stay" and step out on your right foot just as you did in the sit/stay. Count to five and then return to stand beside the dog with him on your left side. Release the treat and praise as always.

Within a week or ten days, you can begin to add a bit of distance between you and your dog when you leave him. When you do, use your left hand open with the palm facing the dog as a stay signal, much the same as the hand signal a police officer uses to stop traffic at an intersection. Hold the food treat in your right hand as before, but this time the food is not touching the dog's nose. He will watch the food hand and quickly learn that he is going to get that treat as soon as you return to his side.

When you can stand 3 feet away from your dog for 30 seconds, you can then begin building time and distance in both stays. Eventually, the dog can be expected to remain in the stay position for prolonged periods of time until you return to him or call him to you. Always praise lavishly when he stays.

Teaching Come

If you make teaching "come" a fun experience, you should never have a student that does not love the game or that fails to come when called. The secret, it seems, is never to teach the word "come." At times when an owner most wants his dog to come when called, the owner is likely to be upset or anxious and he allows these feelings to come through in the tone of his voice when he calls his dog. Hearing that desperation in his owner's voice, the dog fears the results of going to him and therefore either disobeys outright or runs in the opposite direction. The secret, therefore, is to teach the dog a game and, when you want him to come to you, simply play the game. It is practically a no-fail solution!

To begin, have several members of your family take a few food treats and each go into a different room in the house. Take turns calling the dog, and each person should celebrate the dog's finding him with a treat and lots of happy praise. When a person calls the dog, he is actually inviting the dog to find him and get a treat as a reward for "winning."

A few turns of the "Where are you?" game and the dog will understand that everyone is playing the game and that each person has a big celebration awaiting his success at locating them. Once he learns to love the game, simply calling out "Where are you?" will bring him running from wherever he is when he hears that all-important question.

The come command is recognized as one of the most impor-

"WHERE ARE YOU?"

When calling the dog, do not say "Come." Say things like, "Rover, where are you? See if you can find me! I have a biscuit for you!" Keep up a constant line of chatter with coaxing sounds and frequent questions such as, "Where are you?" The dog will learn to follow the sound of your voice to locate you and receive his reward.

tant things to teach a dog, but there are trainers who work with thousands of dogs and never teach the actual word "come." Yet these dogs will race to respond to a person who uses the dog's name followed by "Where are you?" For example, a woman has a 12-year-old companion dog who went blind, but who never fails to locate her owner when asked, "Where are you?"

Children, in particular, love to play this game with their dogs. Children can hide in smaller places like a shower or bathtub, behind a bed or under a table. The dog needs to work a little bit harder to find these hiding places, but, when he does, he loves to celebrate with a treat and a tussle with a favorite youngster.

Walking your dog should be enjoyable, not a battle of wills. Training to heel is essential to make your walks a pleasure.

"COME"... BACK

Never call your dog to come to you for a correction or scold him when he reaches you. That is the quickest way to turn a come command into "Go away fast!" Dogs think only in the present tense, and your dog will connect the scolding with coming to you, not with the misbehavior of a few moments earlier.

Teaching Heel

Heeling means that the dog walks beside the owner without pulling. It takes time and patience on the owner's part to succeed at teaching the dog that he (the owner) will not proceed unless the dog is walking calmly beside him. Pulling out ahead on the lead is definitely not acceptable behavior.

Begin by holding the lead in your left hand as the dog sits beside your left leg. Move the loop end of the lead to your right hand but keep your left hand short on the lead so it keeps the dog in close next to you. Say "Heel" and step forward on your left foot. Keep the dog close to you and take three steps. Stop and have the dog sit next to you in what we now call the heel position. Praise verbally, but do not touch the dog. Hesitate a moment and begin again with "Heel," taking three steps and stopping, at which point the dog is told to sit again.

Your goal here is to have the dog walk those three steps without pulling on the lead. Once he will walk calmly beside you for three steps without pulling, increase the number of steps you take to five. When he will walk politely beside you while you take five steps, you can increase the length of your walk to ten steps. Keep increasing the length of your stroll until the dog will walk quietly beside you without pulling as long as you want him to heel. When you stop heeling, indicate to the dog that the exercise is over by verbally praising as you pet him and say "OK, good dog." The "OK" is used as a release word, meaning that the exercise is finished and the dog is free to relax.

If you are dealing with a dog who insists on pulling you around, simply "put on your brakes" and stand your ground until the dog realizes that the two of you are not going anywhere until he is beside you and moving at your pace, not his. It may take some time just standing there to convince the dog that you are the leader and you will be the one to decide on the direction and speed of your travel.

Each time the dog looks up at you or slows down to give a slack lead between the two of you, quietly praise him and say, "Good heel. Good dog." Eventually, the dog will begin to respond and within a few days he will be walking politely beside you without pulling on the lead. At first, the training sessions should be kept short and very positive; soon the dog will be able to walk nicely with you for increasingly longer distances. Remember also to give the dog free time and the oppor-

Heeling in the show ring is a must, as the dog must respond consistently on lead while the judge assesses his movement.

HEELING WELL

Teach your dog to heel in an enclosed area. Once you think the dog will obey reliably and you want to attempt advanced obedience exercises such as off-lead heeling, test him in a fenced-in area so he cannot run away.

TUG OF WALK?
If you begin teaching the heel by taking long walks and letting the dog pull you along, he misinterprets this action as an acceptable form of taking a walk. When you pull back on the leash to counteract his pulling, he reads that tug as a signal to pull even harder!

tunity to run and play when you have finished heel practice.

WEANING OFF FOOD IN TRAINING

Food is used in training new behaviors. Once the dog understands what behavior goes with a specific command, it is time to start weaning him off the food treats. At first, give a treat after each exercise. Then, start to give a treat only after every other exercise. Mix up the times when you offer a food reward and the times when you only offer praise so that the dog will never know when he is going to receive both food and praise and when he is going to receive only praise. This is called a variable-ratio reward system and it proves successful because there is always the chance that the owner will produce a treat, so the dog never stops trying for that reward. No matter what, *always* give verbal praise.

OBEDIENCE CLASSES

It is a good idea to enroll in an obedience class if one is available in your area. If yours is a show dog, handling classes would be more appropriate. Many areas have dog clubs that offer basic obedience training as well as preparatory classes for obedience competition. There are also local dog trainers who offer similar classes.

At obedience trials, dogs can earn titles at various levels of competition. The beginning levels of competition include basic behaviors such as sit, down, heel, etc. The more advanced levels of competition include jumping, retrieving, scent discrimination and signal work. The advanced levels require a dog and owner to put a lot of time and effort into their training, and the titles that can be earned at these levels of competition are very prestigious.

OTHER ACTIVITIES FOR LIFE

Whether a dog is trained in the structured environment of a class or alone with his owner at home, there are many activities that can bring fun and rewards to both owner and dog once they have mastered basic control.

A BORN PRODIGY

Occasionally, a dog and owner who have not attended formal classes have been able to earn entry-level titles by obtaining competition rules and regulations from a local kennel club and practicing on their own to a degree of perfection. Obtaining the higher level titles, however, almost always requires extensive training under the tutelage of experienced instructors. In addition, the more difficult levels require more specialized equipment whereas the lower levels do not.

Adjustable-height jumps like this are used in trials so that dogs will jump over a height appropriate to their size.

Teaching the dog to help out around the home, in the yard or on the farm provides great satisfaction to both dog and owner. In addition, the dog's help makes life a little easier for his owner and raises his stature as a valued companion to his family. It helps give the dog a purpose by occupying his mind and providing an outlet for his energy.

If you are interested in participating in organized competition with your Toy Manchester, there are activities other than obedience in which you and your dog can become involved. Agility is a popular sport where dogs run through an obstacle course that includes various jumps, tunnels and other exercises to test the dog's speed and coordination. The owners run beside their dogs to give commands and to guide them through the course. Although competitive, the focus is on fun—it's fun to do, fun to watch and great exercise.

PHYSICAL STRUCTURE OF THE TOY MANCHESTER TERRIER

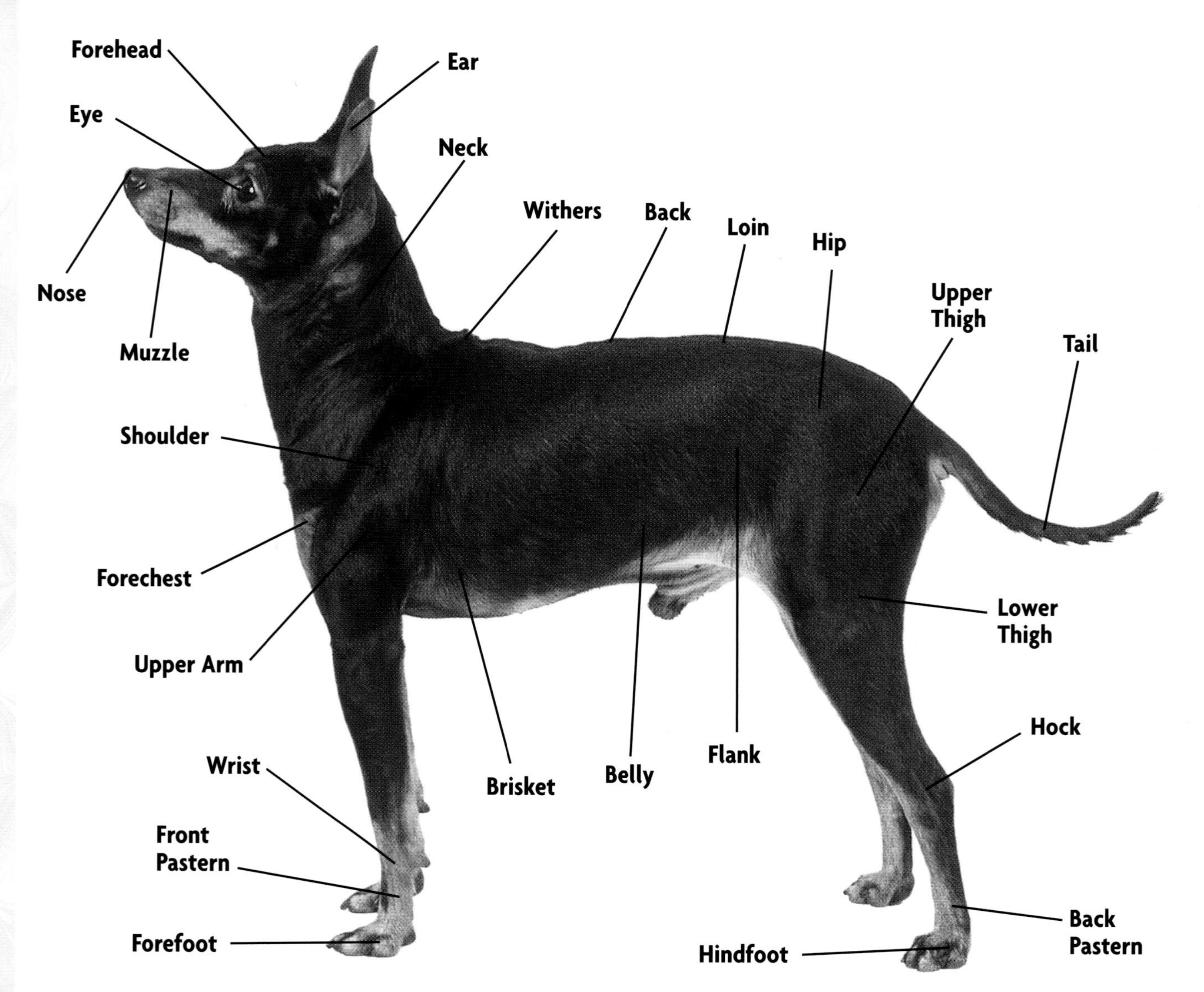

HEALTH CARE OF YOUR
TOY MANCHESTER TERRIER

Dogs suffer from many of the same physical illnesses as people. They might even share many of the same psychological problems. Since people usually know more about human diseases than canine maladies, many of the terms used in this chapter will be familiar but not necessarily those used by veterinarians. We will use the term *x-ray*, instead of the more acceptable term *radiograph*. We will also use the familiar term *symptoms* even though dogs don't have symptoms, which are verbal descriptions of the patient's feelings; dogs have *clinical signs*. Since dogs can't speak, we have to look for clinical signs...but we still use the term *symptoms* in this book.

As a general rule, medicine is *practiced*. That term is not arbitrary. Medicine is a constantly changing art as we learn more and more about genetics, electronic aids (like CAT scans and MRIs) and daily laboratory advances. There are many dog maladies, like canine hip dysplasia, which are not universally treated in the same manner. Some vets opt for surgery more often than others do.

YOUR DOG'S BEST FRIEND

By the time your dog is one year old, you should be very comfortable with your chosen veterinarian and have agreed on scheduled visits for booster vaccinations. Also, your dog's eyes, ears, nose and throat should be examined regularly.

SELECTING A VET

Your selection of a veterinarian should be based upon personality and skills with small dogs as well as upon convenience to your home. You want a vet who is close because you might have emergencies or need to make multiple visits for treatments. You want a vet who has services that you might require such as tattooing and boarding facilities, as well as pet supplies and a good reputation for ability and responsiveness. There is nothing more frustrating than having to wait a day or more to get a response from your vet.

All vets are licensed and their diplomas and/or certificates should be displayed in their waiting rooms. Most vets deal with

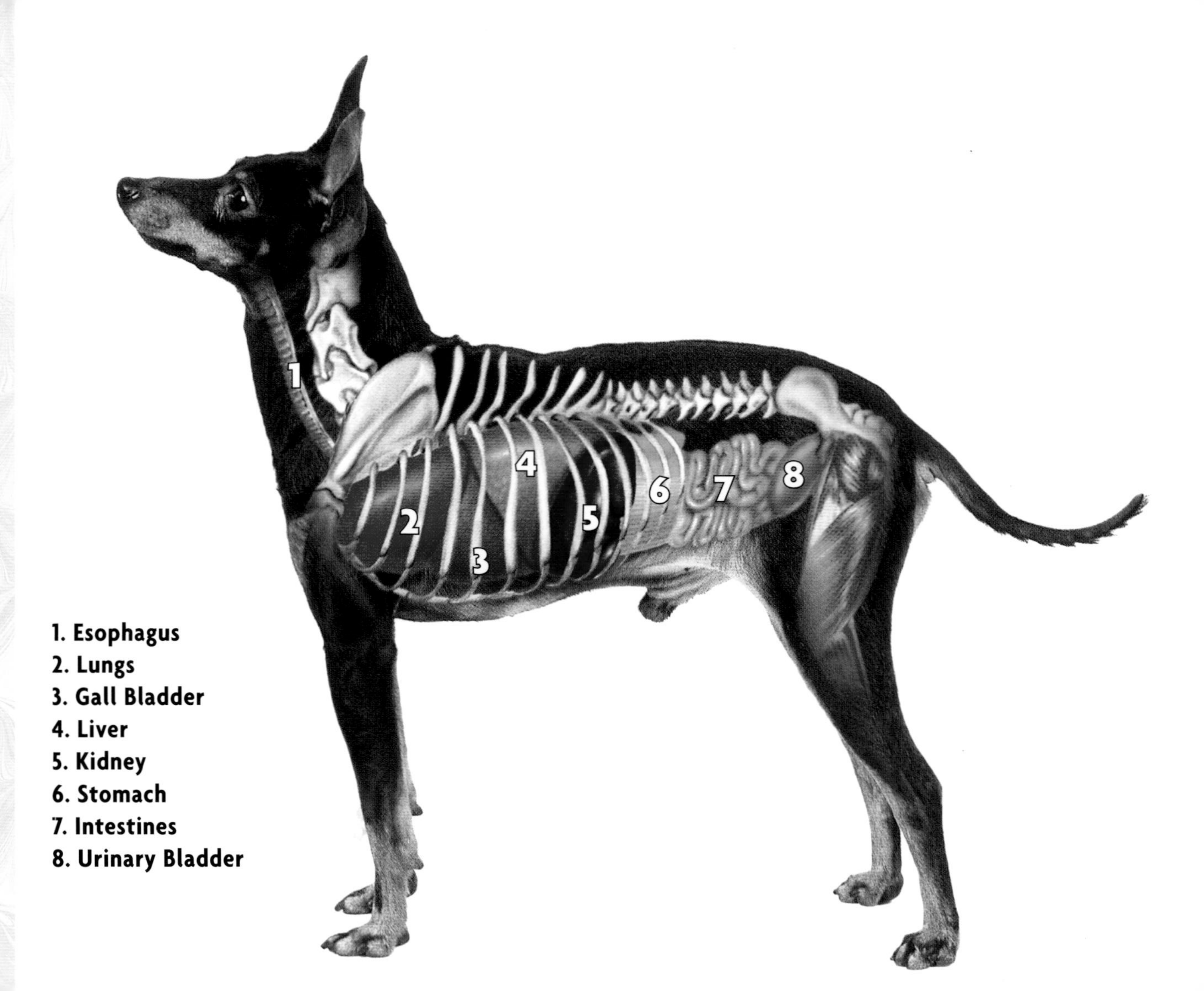

INTERNAL ORGANS OF THE TOY MANCHESTER TERRIER

routine health issues such as checkups, vaccinations, infections, injuries, routine surgery and advising owners about proper health care. There are, however, many veterinary specialties that require further studies and internships. For example, there are specialists in heart problems (veterinary cardiologists), skin problems (veterinary dermatologists), teeth and gum problems (veterinary dentists), eye problems (veterinary ophthalmologists) and x-rays (veterinary radiologists), as well as vets who have specialties in bones, muscles or certain organs. Your vet will refer you to a specialist in the appropriate field when necessary. When the problem affecting your dog is serious, it is not unusual or impudent to get another medical opinion, although it is courteous to advise the vets concerned. You might also want to compare costs among several veterinarians. Sophisticated health care and veterinary services can be very costly. If there is more than one treatment option, financial considerations may play a role in your decision.

PREVENTATIVE MEDICINE

It is much easier, less costly and more effective to practice preventative medicine than to fight bouts of illness and disease. Properly bred puppies come from parents who were selected based upon their genetic-disease profiles.

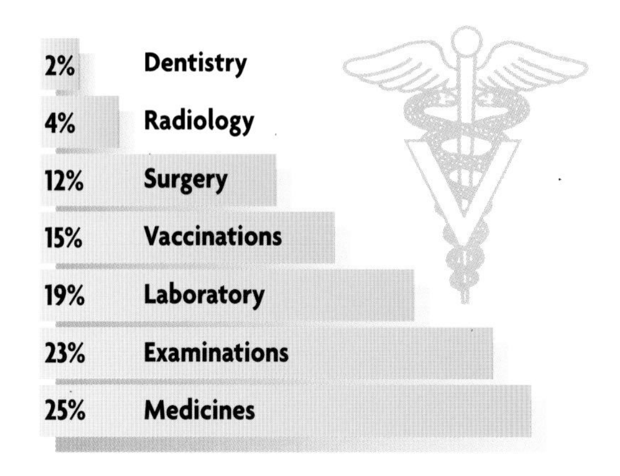

A typical vet's income, categorized according to services performed. This survey dealt with small-animal (pets) practices.

Their mother should have been vaccinated, free of all internal and external parasites and properly nourished. For these reasons, a visit to the vet who cared for the dam is recommended. The dam can pass on disease resistance to her puppies, which can last for eight to ten weeks. She can also pass on parasites and many infections. That's why you should learn as much about the dam's health as possible.

VACCINATION SCHEDULING

Most vaccinations are given by injection and should only be done by a vet. From the onset of your relationship with your vet, be sure to advise him that Toy Manchesters can be particularly sensitive to inoculations and other injections. Both he and you should keep a record of the date of the injection, the identification of the

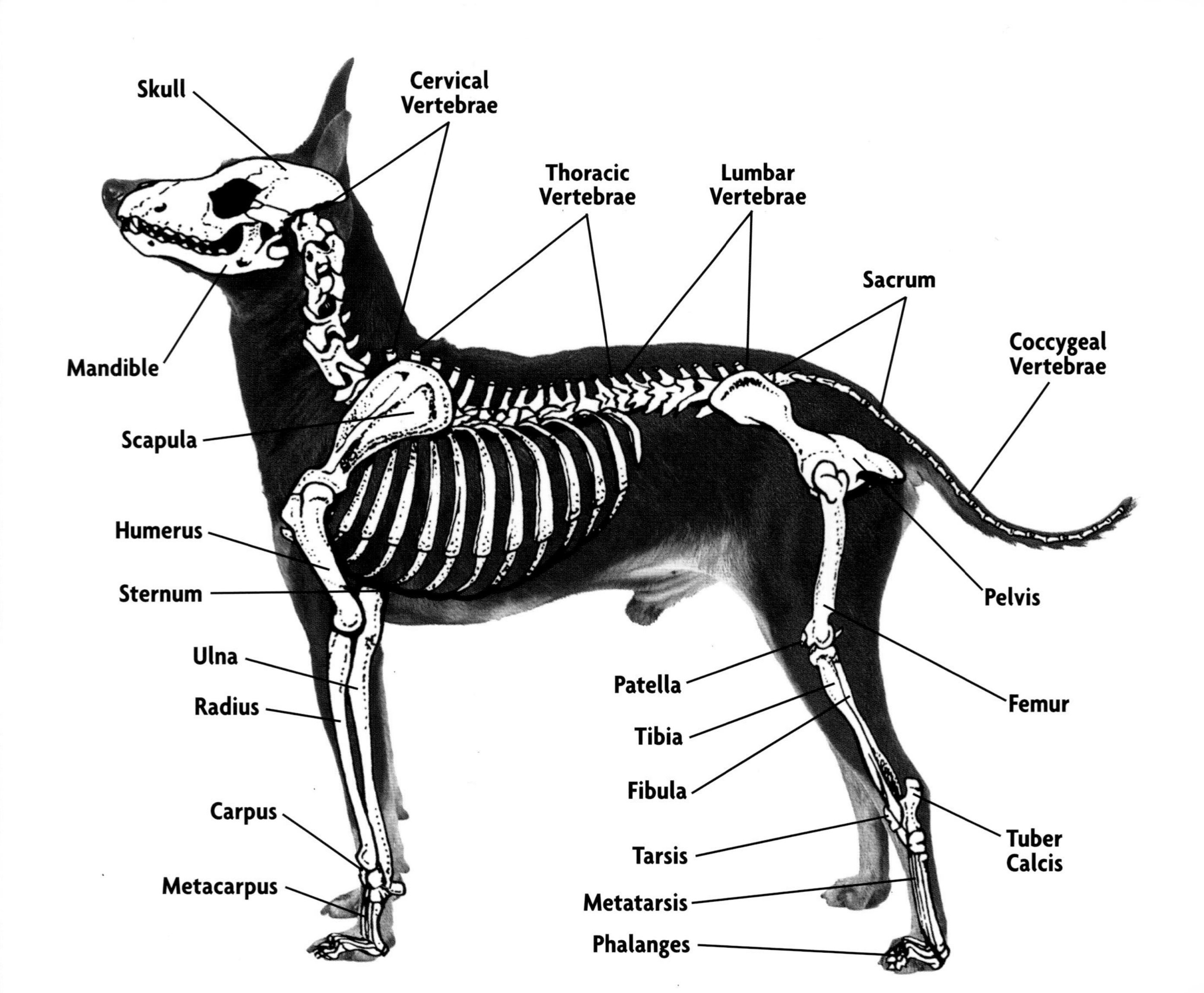

SKELETAL STRUCTURE OF THE TOY MANCHESTER TERRIER

vaccine and the amount given. Some vets give a first vaccination at six weeks, but most dog breeders prefer the course not to commence until about eight weeks because of negating any antibodies passed on by the dam. The vaccination scheduling is usually based on a two- to four-week cycle. You must take your vet's advice regarding when to vaccinate as this may differ according to the vaccine used.

Most vaccinations immunize your puppy against viruses. The usual vaccines contain immunizing doses of several different viruses such as distemper, parvovirus, parainfluenza and hepatitis although some vets recommend separate vaccines for each disease. There are other vaccines available when the puppy is at risk. You should rely

MORE THAN VACCINES

Vaccinations help prevent your new puppy from contracting diseases, but they do not cure them. Proper nutrition as well as parasite control keep your dog healthy and less susceptible to many dangerous diseases. Remember that your dog depends on you to ensure his well-being.

HEALTH AND VACCINATION SCHEDULE

AGE IN WEEKS:	6TH	8TH	10TH	12TH	14TH	16TH	20-24TH	52ND
Worm Control	✔	✔	✔	✔	✔	✔	✔	
Neutering							✔	
Heartworm		✔		✔		✔	✔	
Parvovirus	✔		✔		✔		✔	✔
Distemper		✔		✔		✔		✔
Hepatitis		✔		✔		✔		✔
Leptospirosis								✔
Parainfluenza	✔		✔		✔			✔
Dental Examination		✔					✔	✔
Complete Physical		✔					✔	✔
Coronavirus				✔			✔	✔
Canine Cough	✔							
Hip Dysplasia								✔
Rabies							✔	

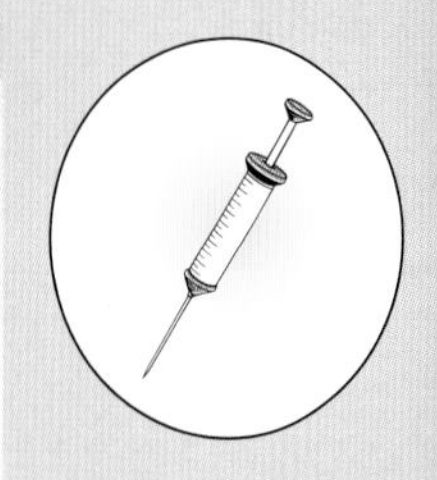

Vaccinations are not instantly effective. It takes about two weeks for the dog's immune system to develop antibodies. Most vaccinations require annual booster shots. Your vet should guide you in this regard.

upon professional advice. This is especially true for the booster-shot program. Most vaccination programs require a booster when the puppy is a year old and once a year thereafter. In some cases, circumstances may require more or less frequent immunizations. Canine cough, more formally known as tracheobronchitis, is treated with a vaccine that is sprayed into the dog's nostrils. Canine cough is usually included in routine vaccination, but this is often not so effective as the other major vaccines.

WEANING TO FIVE MONTHS OLD

Puppies should be weaned by the time they are about two months old. A puppy that remains for at least eight weeks with his dam and littermates usually adapts better to other dogs and people later in life.

Sometimes new owners have their puppy examined by a vet immediately, which is a good idea unless the pup is overtired by the journey home. In that case, an appointment should be made for the next day.

The puppy will have his teeth

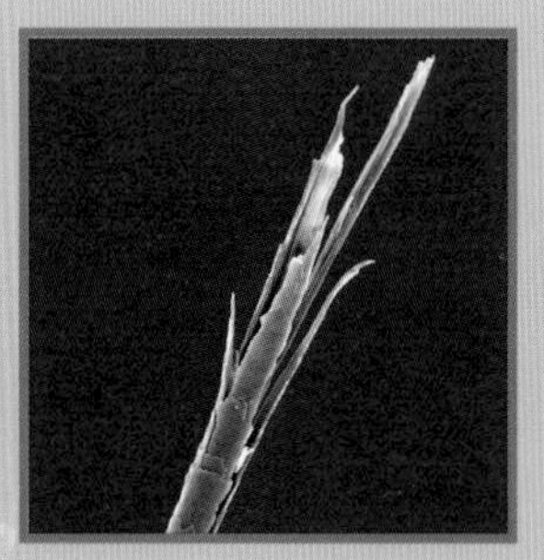

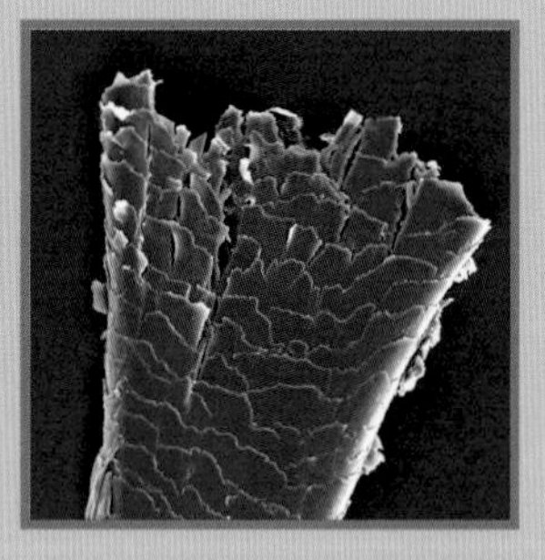

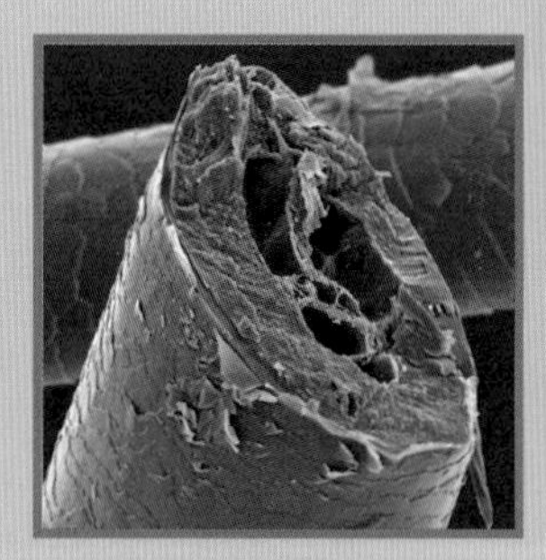

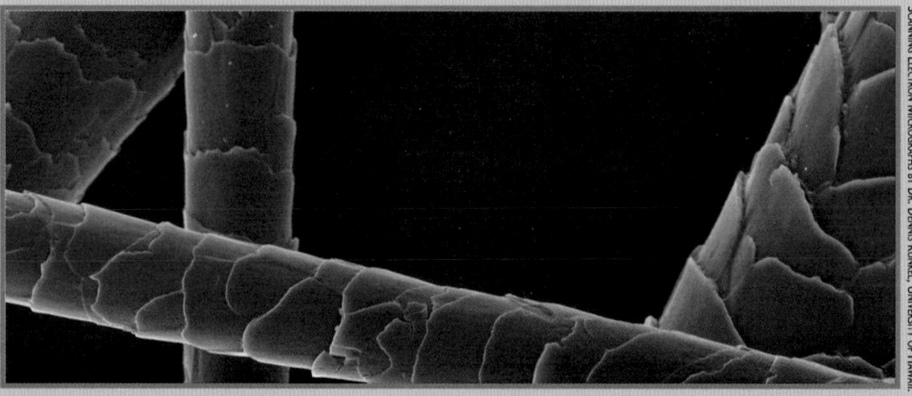

Normal hairs of a dog enlarged 200 times original size. The cuticle (outer covering) is clean and healthy. Unlike human hair that grows from the base, a dog's hair also grows from the end. Damaged hairs and split ends, illustrated above.

Scanning Electron Micrographs by Dr. Dennis Kunkel, University of Hawaii.

DISEASE REFERENCE CHART

	What is it?	What causes it?	Symptoms
Leptospirosis	Severe disease that affects the internal organs; can be spread to people.	A bacterium, which is often carried by rodents, that enters through mucous membranes and spreads quickly throughout the body.	Range from fever, vomiting and loss of appetite in less severe cases to shock, irreversible kidney damage and possibly death in most severe cases.
Rabies	Potentially deadly virus that infects warm-blooded mammals.	Bite from a carrier of the virus, mainly wild animals.	1st stage: dog exhibits change in behavior, fear. 2nd stage: dog's behavior becomes more aggressive. 3rd stage: loss of coordination, trouble with bodily functions.
Parvovirus	Highly contagious virus, potentially deadly.	Ingestion of the virus, which is usually spread through the feces of infected dogs.	Most common: severe diarrhea. Also vomiting, fatigue, lack of appetite.
Canine cough	Contagious respiratory infection.	Combination of types of bacteria and virus. Most common: *Bordetella bronchiseptica* bacteria and parainfluenza virus.	Chronic cough.
Distemper	Disease primarily affecting respiratory and nervous system.	Virus that is related to the human measles virus.	Mild symptoms such as fever, lack of appetite and mucus secretion progress to evidence of brain damage, "hard pad."
Hepatitis	Virus primarily affecting the liver.	Canine adenovirus type I (CAV-1). Enters system when dog breathes in particles.	Lesser symptoms include listlessness, diarrhea, vomiting. More severe symptoms include "blue-eye" (clumps of virus in eye).
Coronavirus	Virus resulting in digestive problems.	Virus is spread through infected dog's feces.	Stomach upset evidenced by lack of appetite, vomiting, diarrhea.

examined and his skeletal conformation and general health checked prior to certification by the vet. Toy Manchester puppies can have problems with their kneecaps and undescended testicles; other common puppy problems include cataracts and heart murmurs. Your vet might have training in temperament evaluation. He also will set up your pup's vaccination schedule.

Five to Twelve Months of Age

Unless you intend to breed or show your dog, neutering the puppy at six months of age is recommended. Discuss this with your vet; neutering/spaying has proven to be extremely beneficial to both male and female dogs. Besides eliminating the possibility of pregnancy and pyometra in bitches and testicular cancer in males, it greatly reduces the risk of (but does not prevent) breast cancer in bitches and prostate cancer in male dogs.

Your vet should provide your puppy with a thorough dental evaluation at six months of age, ascertaining whether all of the permanent teeth have erupted properly. A home dental-care regimen should be initiated at six months, including brushing weekly and providing good dental devices (such as nylon bones). Regular dental care promotes healthy teeth, fresh breath and a longer life.

Older than One Year

Once a year, your full-grown dog should visit the vet for an examination and vaccination boosters, if needed. Some vets recommend blood tests, thyroid level check and dental evaluation to accompany these annual visits. A thorough clinical evaluation by the vet can provide critical background information for your dog. Blood tests are often performed at one year of age, and dental examinations around the third or fourth birthday. In the long run, quality preventative care for your pet can save money, teeth and lives.

VITAL SIGNS

A dog's normal temperature is 101.5 degrees Fahrenheit. A range of between 100.0 and 102.5 degrees should be considered normal, as each dog's body sets its own temperature. It will be helpful if you take your dog's temperature when you know he is healthy and record it. Then, when you suspect that he is not feeling well, you will have a normal figure to compare the abnormal temperature against.

The normal pulse rate for a dog is between 100 and 125 beats per minute.

SKIN PROBLEMS IN TOY MANCHESTERS

Veterinarians are consulted by dog owners for skin problems more than any other group of diseases or maladies. Dogs' skin is almost as sensitive as human skin and both suffer almost the same ailments (though the occurrence of acne in most dogs is rare). For this reason, veterinary dermatology has developed into a specialty practiced by many veterinarians.

Since many skin problems have visual symptoms that are almost identical, it requires the skill of an experienced veterinary dermatologist to identify and cure many of the more severe skin disorders. Pet shops sell many treatments for skin problems, but most of the treatments are directed at symptoms and not the underlying problem(s). If your dog is suffering from a skin disorder, you should seek professional assistance as quickly as possible. As with all diseases, the earlier a problem is identified and treated, the more likely is a complete cure.

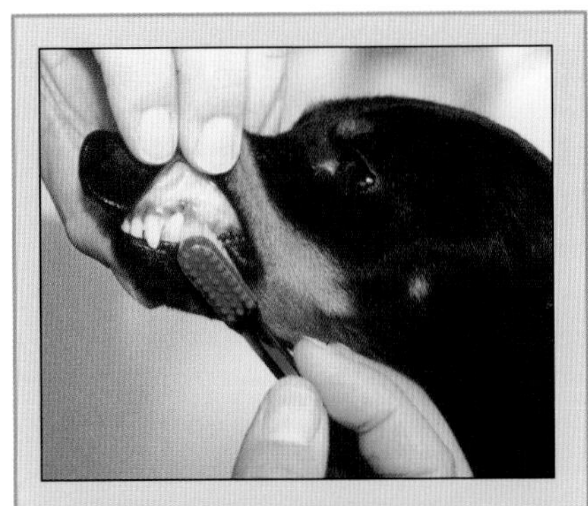

CARETAKER OF TEETH

You are your dog's caretaker and his dentist. Vets warn that plaque and tartar buildup on the teeth will damage the gums and allow bacteria to enter the dog's bloodstream, causing serious damage to the animal's vital organs. Studies show that over 50 percent of dogs have some form of gum disease before age three. Daily or weekly tooth cleaning (with a brush or soft gauze pad wipes) can add to your dog's life.

Hereditary Skin Disorders

Veterinary dermatologists are currently researching a number of skin disorders that are believed to have a hereditary basis. These inherited diseases are transmitted by both parents, who appear (phenotypically) normal but have a recessive gene for the disease, meaning that they carry, but are not affected by, the disease. These diseases pose serious problems to breeders because in some instances there is no method of identifying carriers. Often the secondary diseases associated with these skin conditions are even more debilitating than the disorder itself, including cancers and respiratory problems.

Among the hereditary skin disorders, for which the mode of inheritance is known, are acrodermatitis, cutaneous asthenia (Ehlers-Danlos syndrome), sebaceous adenitis, cyclic hematopoiesis, dermatomyositis, IgA deficiency, color dilution alopecia and nodular dermatofibrosis. Some of these disorders are limited to one or two breeds and others affect a large number of breeds. All inherited diseases must be diagnosed and treated by a veterinary specialist.

Parasite Bites

Many of us are allergic to insect bites. The bites itch, erupt and may even become infected. Dogs have the same reaction to fleas, ticks and/or mites. When an insect lands on you, you have the chance to whisk it away with your hand. Unfortunately, when your dog is bitten by a flea, tick or mite, he can only scratch it away or bite it. By the time the dog has been bitten, the parasite has done some of its damage. It may also have laid eggs to cause further problems in the near future. The itching from parasite bites is probably due to the saliva injected into the site when the parasite sucks the dog's blood.

Auto-Immune Skin Conditions

Auto-immune skin conditions are commonly referred to as being allergic to yourself, while allergies are usually inflammatory reactions to an outside stimulus. Auto-immune diseases cause serious damage to the tissues that are involved.

The best known auto-immune disease is lupus, which affects people as well as dogs. The symptoms are variable and may affect the kidneys, bones, blood chemistry and skin. It can be fatal to both dogs and humans, though it is not thought to be transmissible. It is usually successfully treated with cortisone, prednisone or a similar corticosteroid, but extensive use of these drugs can have harmful side effects.

"P" STANDS FOR PROBLEM

Urinary tract disease is a serious condition that requires immediate medical attention. Symptoms include urinating in inappropriate places or the need to urinate frequently in small amounts. Urinary-tract disease is most effectively treated with antibiotics. To help promote good urinary-tract health, owners must always be sure that a constant supply of fresh water is available to their pets.

Airborne Allergies

Just as humans have hay fever, rose fever and other fevers from which they suffer during the pollinating season, many dogs suffer from the same allergies. When the pollen count is high, your dog might suffer, but don't expect him to sneeze and have a runny nose like a human would. Dogs react to pollen allergies the same way they react to fleas—they scratch and bite themselves.

Dogs, like humans, can be tested for allergens. Discuss the testing with your veterinary dermatologist.

FOOD PROBLEMS

Food Allergies

Dogs are allergic to many foods that are best-sellers and highly recommended by breeders and vets. Changing the brand of food that you buy may not eliminate the problem if the element to which the dog is allergic is contained in the new brand.

Recognizing a food allergy is difficult. Humans vomit or have rashes when they eat a food to which they are allergic. Dogs neither vomit nor (usually) develop a rash. They react in the same manner as they do to an airborne or flea allergy; they itch, scratch and bite, thus making the diagnosis extremely difficult. While pollen allergies and parasite bites are usually seasonal, food allergies are year-round problems.

Food Intolerance

Food intolerance is the inability of the dog to completely digest certain foods. For example, puppies that may have done very well on their mother's milk may not do well on cow's milk. The result of this food intolerance may be loose bowels, passing gas and stomach pains. These are the only symptoms of food intolerance and that makes diagnosis difficult.

Treating Food Problems

It is possible to handle food allergies and food intolerance yourself. Put your dog on a diet that he has never had. Obviously, if he has never eaten this new food, he can't yet have been allergic or intolerant of it. Start with a single ingredient that is not in the dog's diet at the present time. Ingredients like chopped beef or chicken are common in dogs' diets, so try another quality protein source like fish, lamb or something more exotic like rabbit or pheasant. Keep the dog on this diet (with no additives) for a month. If the symptoms of food allergy or intolerance disappear, chances are your dog has a food allergy.

Don't think that the single ingredient cured the problem. You still must find a suitable diet and ascertain which ingredient in the old diet was objectionable. This is most easily done by adding ingredients to the new diet one at a time. Let the dog stay on the modified diet for a month before you add another ingredient. Eventually, you will determine the ingredient that caused the adverse reaction.

An alternative method is to carefully study the ingredients in the diet to which your dog is allergic or intolerant. Identify the main ingredient in this diet and eliminate the main ingredient by buying a different food that does not have that ingredient. Keep experimenting until the symptoms disappear after one month on the new diet.

PET ADVANTAGES

If you do not intend to show or breed your new puppy, your veterinarian will probably recommend that you spay your female or neuter your male. Some people believe neutering leads to weight gain, but if you feed and exercise your dog properly, this is easily avoided. Spaying or neutering can actually have many positive outcomes, such as:

- training becomes easier, as the dog focuses less on the urge to mate and more on you!
- females are protected from unplanned pregnancy as well as ovarian and uterine cancers.
- males are guarded from testicular tumors and have a reduced risk of developing prostate cancer.

Talk to your vet regarding the right age to spay/neuter and other aspects of the procedure.

A male dog flea, *Ctenocephalides canis.*

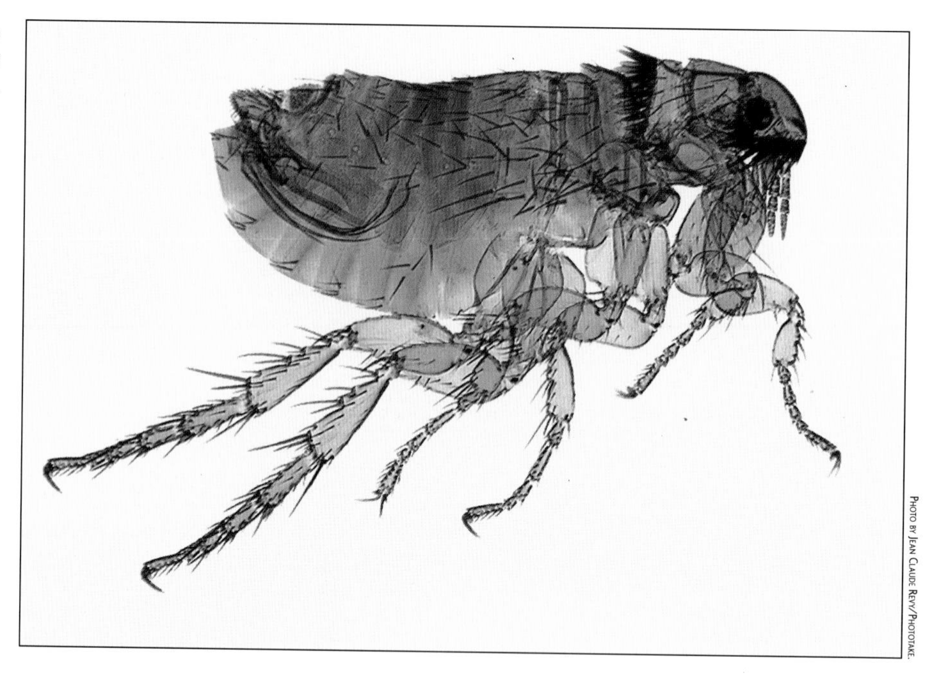

PHOTO BY JEAN CLAUDE REVY/PHOTOTAKE.

EXTERNAL PARASITES

FLEAS

Of all the problems to which dogs are prone, none is more well known and frustrating than fleas. Flea infestation is relatively simple to cure but difficult to prevent. Parasites that are harbored inside the body are a bit more difficult to eradicate but they are easier to control.

To control flea infestation, you have to understand the flea's life cycle. Fleas are often thought of as a summertime problem, but centrally heated homes have changed the patterns and fleas can be found at any time of the year. The most effective method of flea control is a two-stage approach: one stage to kill the adult fleas, and the other to control the development of pre-adult fleas. Unfortunately, no single active ingredient is effective against all stages of the life cycle.

FLEA KILLER CAUTION—"POISON"

Flea-killers are poisonous. You should not spray these toxic chemicals on areas of a dog's body that he licks, including his genitals and his face. Flea killers taken internally are a better answer, but check with your vet in case internal therapy is not advised for your dog.

Life Cycle Stages

During its life, a flea will pass through four life stages: egg, larva, pupa or nymph and adult. The adult stage is the most visible and irritating stage of the flea life cycle, and this is why the majority of flea-control products concentrate on this stage. The fact is that adult fleas account for only 1% of the total flea population, and the other 99% exist in pre-adult stages, i.e., eggs, larvae and nymphs. The pre-adult stages are barely visible to the naked eye.

The Life Cycle of the Flea

Eggs are laid on the dog, usually in quantities of about 20 or 30, several times a day. The adult female flea must have a blood meal before each egg-laying session. When first laid, the eggs will cling to the dog's hair, as the eggs are still moist. However, they will quickly dry out and fall from the dog, especially if the dog moves around or scratches. Many eggs will fall off in the dog's favorite area or an area in which he spends a lot of time, such as his bed.

Once the eggs fall from the dog onto the carpet or furniture, they will hatch into larvae. This takes from one to ten days. Larvae are not particularly mobile and will usually travel only a few inches from where they hatch. However, they do have a tendency to move away from bright light and heavy traffic—under furniture and behind doors are common places to find high quantities of flea larvae.

The flea larvae feed on dead organic matter, including adult flea feces, until they are ready to change into adult fleas. Fleas will usually remain as larvae for around seven days. After this period, the larvae will pupate into protective pupae. While inside the pupae, the larvae will undergo metamorphosis and change into

EN GARDE:
CATCHING FLEAS OFF GUARD!

Consider the following ways to arm yourself against fleas:

- Add a small amount of pennyroyal or eucalyptus oil to your dog's bath. These natural remedies repel fleas.
- Supplement your dog's food with fresh garlic (minced or grated) and a hearty amount of brewer's yeast, both of which ward off fleas.
- Use a flea comb on your dog daily. Submerge fleas in a cup of bleach to kill them quickly.
- Confine the dog to only a few rooms to limit the spread of fleas in the home.
- Vacuum daily...and get all of the crevices! Dispose of the bag every few days until the problem is under control.
- Wash your dog's bedding daily. Cover cushions where your dog sleeps with towels, and wash the towels often.

Fleas have been measured as being able to jump 300,000 times and can jump over 150 times their length in any direction, including straight up.

adult fleas. This can take as little time as a few days, but the adult fleas can remain inside the pupae waiting to hatch for up to two years. The pupae are signaled to hatch by certain stimuli, such as physical pressure—the pupae's being stepped on, heat from an animal's lying on the pupae or increased carbon-dioxide levels and vibrations—indicating that a suitable host is available.

Once hatched, the adult flea must feed within a few days. Once the adult flea finds a host, it will not leave voluntarily. It only becomes dislodged by grooming or the host animal's scratching. The adult flea will remain on the host for the duration of its life unless forcibly removed.

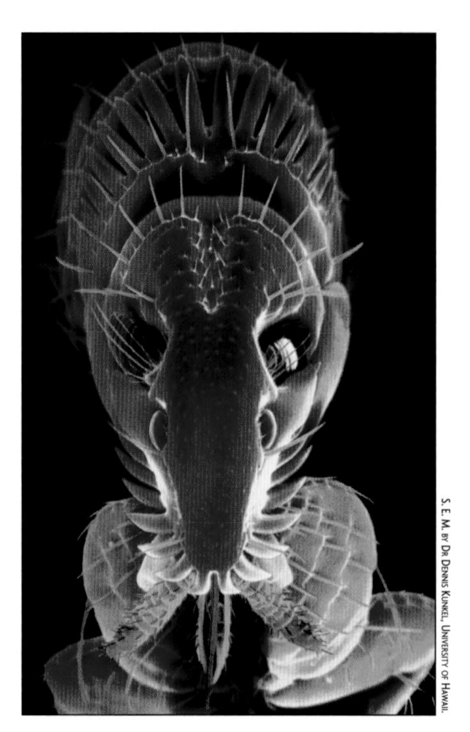

A scanning electron micrograph of a dog or cat flea, *Ctenocephalides*, magnified more than 100x. This image has been colorized for effect.

S.E.M. by Dr Dennis Kunkel, University of Hawaii.

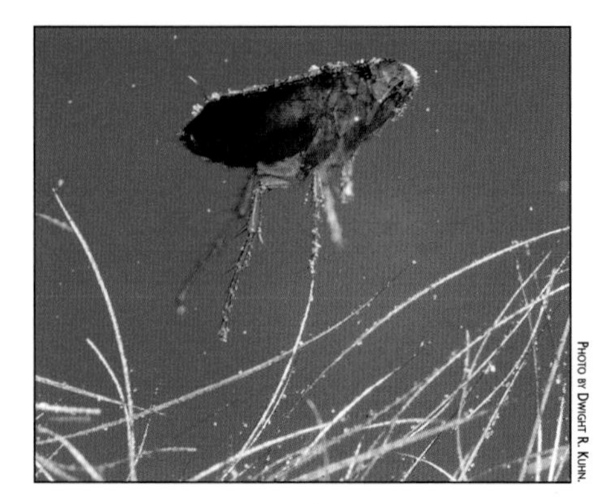

Photo by Dwight R. Kuhn.

Treating the Environment and the Dog

Treating fleas should be a two-pronged attack. First, the environment needs to be treated; this includes carpets and furniture, especially the dog's bedding and areas underneath furniture. The environment should be treated with a household spray containing an Insect Growth Regulator (IGR) and an insecticide to kill the adult fleas. Most IGRs are effective against eggs and larvae; they actually mimic the fleas' own hormones and stop the eggs and larvae from developing into adult fleas. There are currently no treatments available to attack the pupa stage of the life cycle, so the adult insecticide is used to kill the newly hatched adult fleas before they find a host. Most IGRs are active for many months, while adult insecticides are only active

THE LIFE CYCLE OF THE FLEA

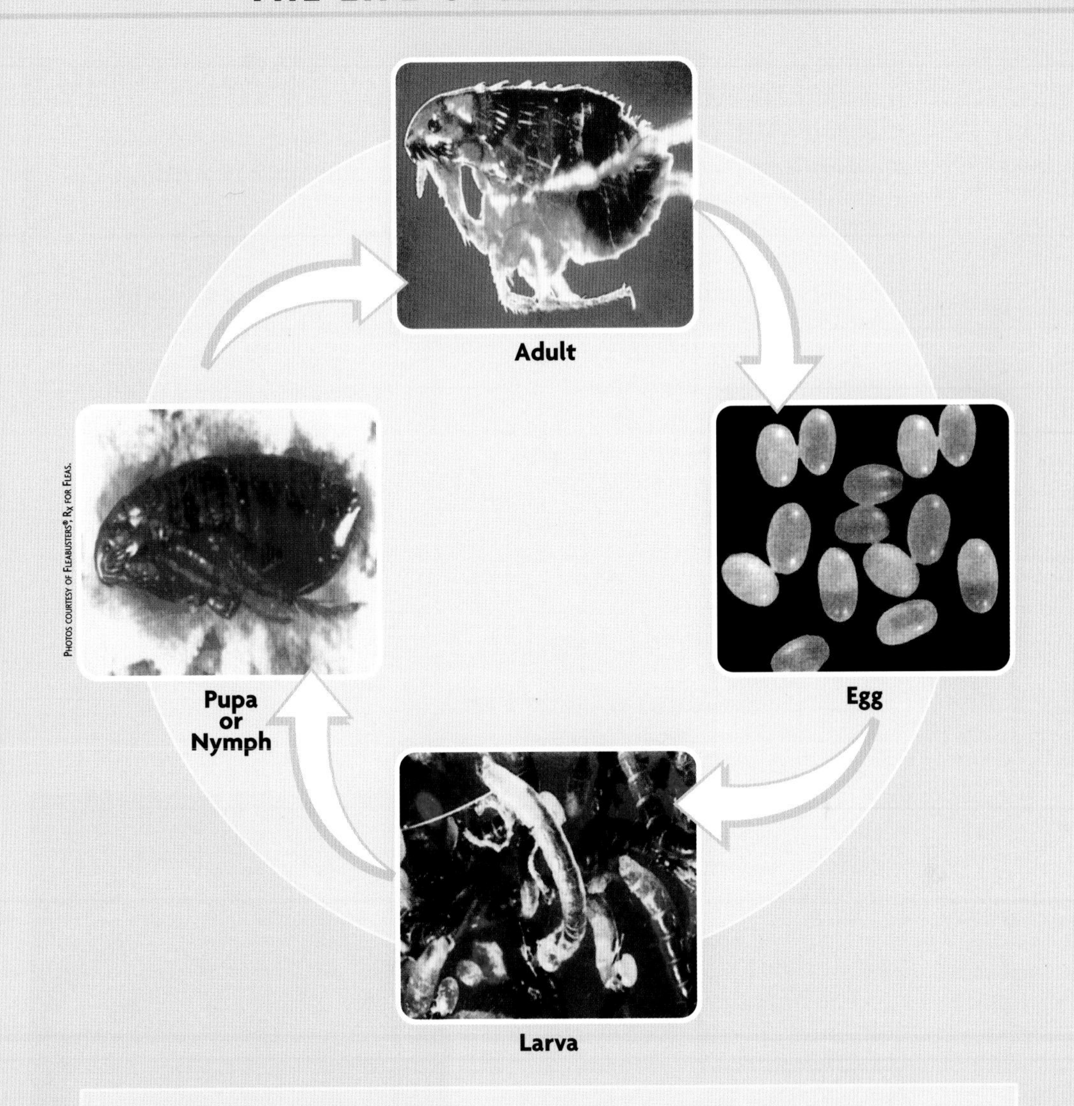

Fleas have been around for millions of years and have adapted to changing host animals. They are able to go through a complete life cycle in less than one month or they can extend their lives to almost two years by remaining as pupae or cocoons. They do not need blood or any other food for up to 20 months.

INSECT GROWTH REGULATOR (IGR)

Two types of products should be used when treating fleas—a product to treat the pet and a product to treat the home. Adult fleas represent less than 1% of the flea population. The pre-adult fleas (eggs, larvae and pupae) represent more than 99% of the flea population and are found in the environment; it is in the case of pre-adult fleas that products containing an Insect Growth Regulator (IGR) should be used in the home.

IGRs are a new class of compounds used to prevent the development of insects. They do not kill the insect outright, but instead use the insect's biology against it to stop it from completing its growth. Products that contain methoprene are the world's first and leading IGRs. Used to control fleas and other insects, this type of IGR will stop flea larvae from developing and protect the house for up to seven months.

for a few days.

When treating with a household spray, it is a good idea to vacuum before applying the product. This stimulates as many pupae as possible to hatch into adult fleas. The vacuum cleaner should also be treated with an insecticide to prevent the eggs and larvae that have been collected in the vacuum bag from hatching.

The second stage of treatment is to apply an adult insecticide to the dog. Traditionally, this would be in the form of a collar or a spray, but more recent innovations include digestible insecticides that poison the fleas when they ingest the dog's blood. Alternatively, there are drops that, when placed on the back of the dog's neck, spread throughout the hair and skin to kill adult fleas.

TICKS

Though not as common as fleas, ticks are found all over the tropical and temperate world. They don't bite, like fleas; they harpoon. They dig their sharp proboscis (nose) into the dog's skin and drink the blood. Their only food and drink is dog's

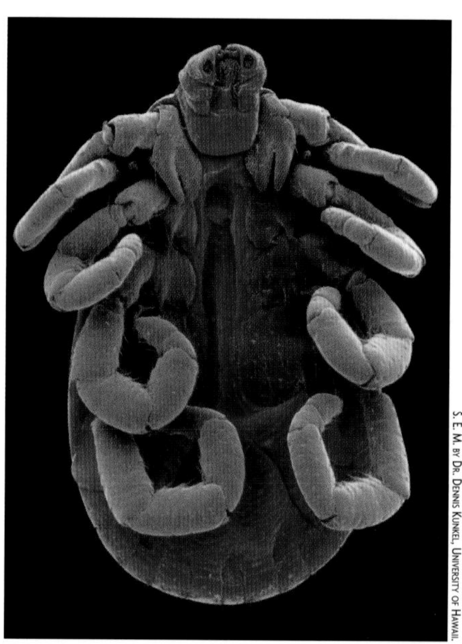

S.E.M. by Dr. Dennis Kunkel, University of Hawaii.

The American dog tick, *Dermacentor variabilis*, is probably the most common tick found on dogs. Look at the strength in its eight legs! No wonder it's hard to detach them.

blood. Dogs can get Lyme disease, Rocky Mountain spotted fever, tick bite paralysis and many other diseases from ticks. They may live where fleas are found and they like to hide in cracks or seams in walls. They are controlled the same way fleas are controlled.

The American dog tick, *Dermacentor variabilis*, may well be the most common dog tick in many geographical areas, especially those areas where the climate is hot and humid. Most dog ticks have life expectancies of a week to six months, depending upon climatic conditions. They can neither jump nor fly, but they can crawl slowly and can range up to 16 feet to reach a sleeping or unsuspecting dog.

DEER-TICK CROSSING

The great outdoors may be fun for your dog, but it also is a home to dangerous ticks. Deer ticks carry a bacterium known as *Borrelia burgdorferi* and are most active in the autumn and spring. When infections are caught early, penicillin and tetracycline are effective antibiotics, but, if left untreated, the bacteria may cause neurological, kidney and cardiac problems as well as long-term trouble with walking and painful joints.

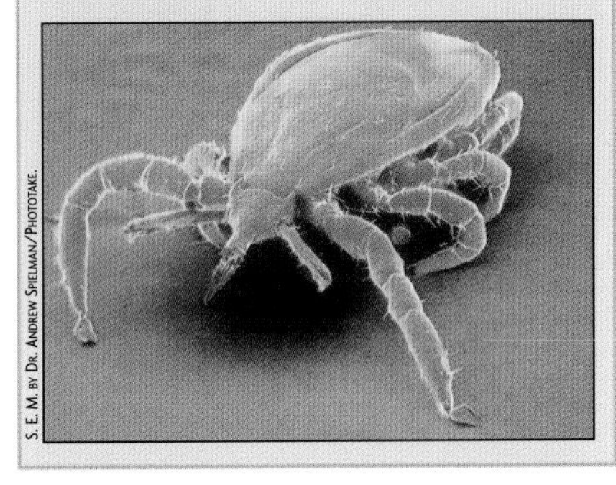

S. E. M. by Dr. Andrew Spielman/Phototake.

Mites

Just as fleas and ticks can be problematic for your dog, mites can also lead to an itchy nuisance. Microscopic in size, mites are related to ticks and generally take up permanent residence on their host animal—in this case, your dog! The term *mange* refers to any infestation caused by one of the mighty mites, of which there are six varieties that concern dog owners.

Demodex mites cause a condition known as demodicosis (sometimes called red mange or

Photo by Dr. Dennis Kunkel, University of Hawaii.

The head of an American dog tick, *Dermacentor variabilis*, enlarged and colorized for effect.

The mange mite, *Psoroptes bovis*, can infest cattle and other domestic animals.

PHOTO BY JAMES HAYDEN/YOAV/PHOTOTAKE.

follicular mange), in which the mites live in the dog's hair follicles and sebaceous glands in larger-than-normal numbers. This type of mange is commonly passed from the dam to her puppies and usually shows up on the puppies' muzzles, though demodicosis is not transferable from one normal dog to another. Most dogs recover from this type of mange without any treatment, though topical therapies are commonly prescribed by the vet.

Human lice look like dog lice; the two are closely related.

PHOTO BY DWIGHT R. KUHN.

The *Cheyletiellosis* mite is the hook-mouthed culprit associated with "walking dandruff," a condition that affects dogs as well as cats and rabbits. This mite lives on the surface of the animal's skin and is readily transferable through direct or indirect contact with an affected animal. The dandruff is present in the form of scaly skin, which may or may not be itchy. If not treated, this mange can affect a whole kennel of dogs and can be spread to humans as well.

The *Sarcoptes* mite causes intense itching on the dog in the form of a condition known as scabies or sarcoptic mange. The cycle of the *Sarcoptes* mite lasts about three weeks, and the mites live in the top layer of the dog's skin (epidermis), preferably in areas with little hair. Scabies is highly contagious and can be passed to humans. Sometimes an allergic reaction to the mite worsens the severe itching associated with sarcoptic mange.

Ear mites, *Otodectes cynotis,* lead to otodectic mange, which most commonly affects the outer ear canal of the dog, though other areas can be affected as well. Dogs with ear-mite infestation commonly scratch at their ears, causing further irritation, and shake their heads. Dark brown droppings in the outer ear confirm the diagnosis. Your vet can prescribe a treatment to flush out the ears and kill any eggs in the ears. A complete month of treatment is necessary to cure the mange.

Two other mites, less common in dogs, include *Dermanyssus gallinae* (the poultry or red mite) and *Eutrombicula alfreddugesi* (the North American mite associated with trombiculidiasis or chigger infestation). The poultry mite frequently lives on chickens, but can transfer to dogs who spend time near farm animals. Chigger infestation affects dogs in the Central US who have exposure to woodlands. The types of mange caused by both of these mites are treatable by vets.

DO NOT MIX

Never mix parasite-control products without first consulting your vet. Some products can become toxic when combined with others and can cause fatal consequences.

NOT A DROP TO DRINK

Never allow your dog to swim in polluted water or public areas where water quality can be suspect. Even perfectly clear water can harbor parasites, many of which can cause serious to fatal illnesses in canines. Areas inhabited by waterfowl and other wildlife are especially dangerous.

INTERNAL PARASITES

Most animals—fishes, birds and mammals, including dogs and humans—have worms and other parasites that live inside their bodies. According to Dr. Herbert R. Axelrod, the fish pathologist, there are two kinds of parasites: dumb and smart. The smart parasites live in peaceful cooperation with their hosts (symbiosis), while the dumb parasites kill their hosts. Most worm infections are relatively easy to control. If they are not controlled, they weaken the host dog to the point that other medical problems occur, but they do not kill the host as dumb parasites would.

A brown dog tick, *Rhipicephalus sanguineus*, is an uncommon but annoying tick found on dogs.

Photo by Carolina Biological Supply/Phototake.

The roundworm *Rhabditis* can infect both dogs and humans.

ROUNDWORMS

Average-size dogs can pass 1,360,000 roundworm eggs every day. For example, if there were only 1 million dogs in the world, the world would be saturated with thousands of tons of dog feces. These feces would contain around 15,000,000,000 roundworm eggs.

Up to 31% of home yards and children's sand boxes in the US contain roundworm eggs.

Flushing dog's feces down the toilet is not a safe practice because the usual sewage treatments do not destroy roundworm eggs.

Infected puppies start shedding roundworm eggs at three weeks of age. They can be infected by their mother's milk.

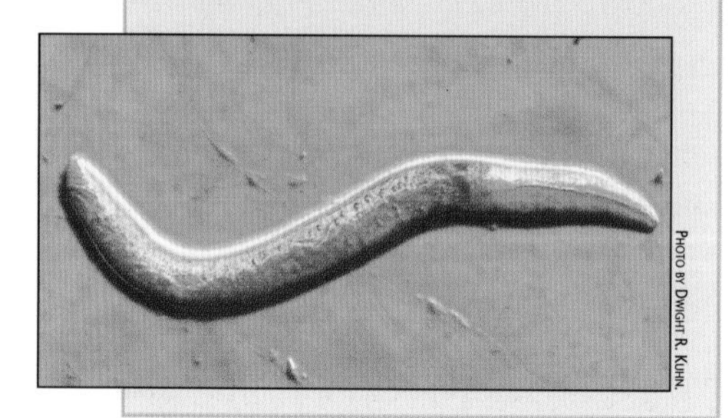

The roundworm, *Ascaris lumbricoides.*

Roundworms

The roundworms that infect dogs are known scientifically as *Toxocara canis.* They live in the dog's intestines and shed eggs continually. It has been estimated that a dog produces about 6 or more ounces of feces every day. Each ounce of feces averages hundreds of thousands of roundworm eggs. There are no known areas in which dogs roam that do not contain roundworm eggs. The greatest danger of roundworms is that they infect people, too! It is wise to have your dog tested regularly for roundworms.

In young puppies, roundworms cause bloated bellies, diarrhea, coughing and vomiting, and are transmitted from the dam (through blood or milk). Affected puppies will not appear as animated as normal puppies. The worms appear spaghetti-like, measuring as long as 6 inches. Adult dogs can acquire roundworms through coprophagia (eating contaminated feces) or by killing rodents that carry roundworms.

Roundworm infection can kill puppies and cause severe problems in adults, as the hatched larvae travel to the lungs and trachea through the bloodstream. Cleanliness is the best preventative for roundworms. Always pick up after your dog and dispose of feces in appropriate receptacles.

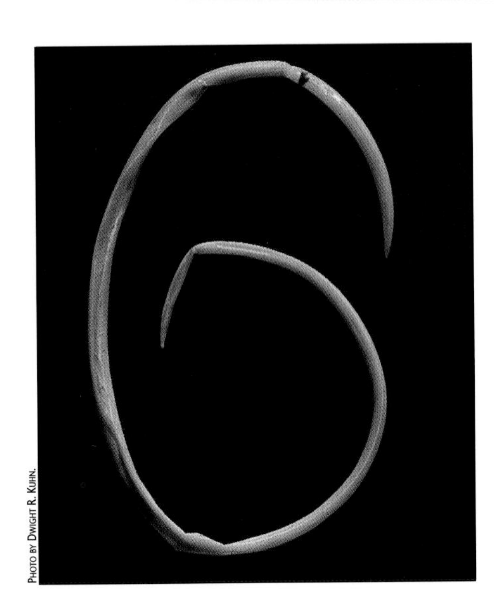

The hookworm, *Ancylostoma caninum.*

HOOKWORMS

In the United States, dog owners have to be concerned about four different species of hookworm, the most common and most serious of which is *Ancylostoma caninum,* which prefers warm climates. The others are *Ancylostoma braziliense, Ancylostoma tubaeforme* and *Uncinaria stenocephala,* the latter of which is a concern to dogs living in the Northern US and Canada, as this species prefers cold climates. Hookworms are dangerous to humans as well as to dogs and cats, and can be the cause of severe anemia due to iron deficiency. The worm uses its teeth to attach itself to the dog's intestines and changes the site of its attachment about six times per day. Each time the worm repositions itself, the dog loses blood and can become anemic. *Ancylostoma caninum* is the most likely of the four species to cause anemia in the dog.

Symptoms of hookworm infection include dark stools, weight loss, general weakness, pale coloration and anemia, as well as possible skin problems. Fortunately, hookworms are easily purged from the affected dog with a number of medications that have proven effective. Discuss these with your vet. Most heartworm preventatives include a hookworm insecticide as well.

Owners also must be aware that hookworms can infect humans, who can acquire the larvae through exposure to contaminated feces. Since the worms cannot complete their life cycle on a human, the worms simply infest the skin and cause irritation. This condition is known as cutaneous larva migrans syndrome. As a preventative, use disposable gloves or a "poop-scoop" to pick up your dog's droppings and prevent your dog (or neighborhood cats) from defecating in children's play areas.

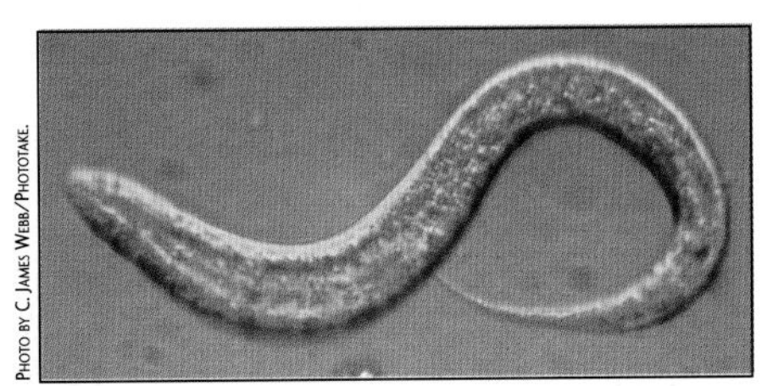

The infective stage of the hookworm larva.

TAPEWORMS

Humans, rats, squirrels, foxes, coyotes, wolves and domestic dogs are all susceptible to tapeworm infection. Except in humans, tapeworms are usually not a fatal infection. Infected individuals can harbor 1000 parasitic worms.

Tapeworms, like some other types of worm, are hermaphroditic, meaning male and female in the same worm.

If dogs eat infected rats or mice, or anything else infected with tapeworm, they get the tapeworm disease. One month after attaching to a dog's intestine, the worm starts shedding eggs. These eggs are infective immediately. Infective eggs can live for a few months without a host animal.

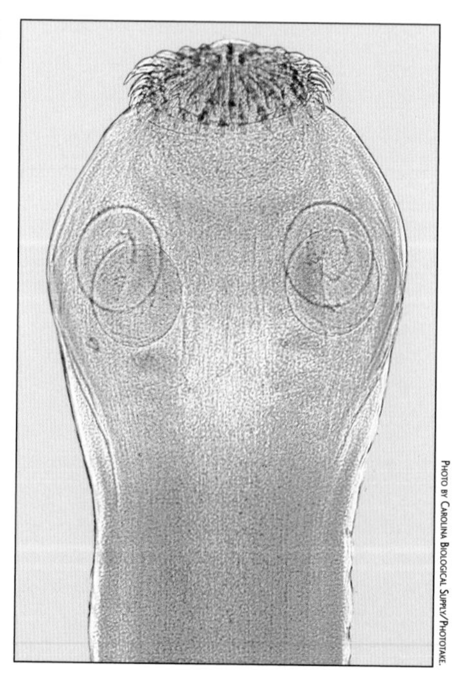

The head and rostellum (the round prominence on the scolex) of a tapeworm, which infects dogs and humans.

PHOTO BY CAROLINA BIOLOGICAL SUPPLY/PHOTOTAKE.

TAPEWORMS

There are many species of tapeworm, all of which are carried by fleas! The most common tapeworm affecting dogs is known as *Dipylidium caninum*. The dog eats the flea and starts the tapeworm cycle. Humans can also be infected with tapeworms—so don't eat fleas! Fleas are so small that your dog could pass them onto your hands, your plate or your food and thus make it possible for you to ingest a flea that is carrying tapeworm eggs.

While tapeworm infection is not life-threatening in dogs (smart parasite!), it can be the cause of a very serious liver disease for humans. About 50% of the humans infected with *Echinococcus multilocularis*, a type of tapeworm that causes alveolar hydatid, perish.

WHIPWORMS

In North America, whipworms are counted among the most common parasitic worms in dogs. The whipworm's scientific name is *Trichuris vulpis*. These worms attach themselves in the lower parts of the intestine, where they feed. Affected dogs may only experience upset tummies, colic and diarrhea. These worms, however, can live for months or years in the dog, beginning their larval stage in the small intestine, spending their adult stage in the large intestine and finally passing infective eggs through the dog's feces. The only way to detect whipworms is through a fecal examination, though this is not always foolproof. Treatment for whipworms is tricky, due to the worms' unusual life-cycle pattern, and very often dogs are reinfected due to exposure to infective eggs on the ground. The whipworm eggs can survive in the environment for as long as five years; thus, cleaning up droppings in your own backyard as well as in public places is absolutely essential for sanitation purposes and the health of your dog and others.

THREADWORMS

Though less common than roundworms, hookworms and those previously mentioned, threadworms concern dog owners in the Southwestern US and Gulf Coast area where the climate is hot and humid. Living in the small intestine of the dog, this worm measures a mere 2 millimeters and is round in shape. Like that of the whipworm, the threadworm's life cycle is very complex and the eggs and larvae are passed through the feces. A deadly disease in humans, *Strongyloides* readily infects people, and the handling of feces is the most common means of transmission. Threadworms are most often seen in young puppies; bloody diarrhea and pneumonia are symptoms. Sick puppies must be isolated and treated immediately; vets recommend a follow-up treatment one month later.

HEARTWORM PREVENTATIVES

There are many heartworm preventatives on the market, many of which are sold at your veterinarian's office. These products can be given daily or monthly, depending on the manufacturer's instructions. All of these preventatives contain chemical insecticides directed at killing heartworms, which leads to some controversy among dog owners. In effect, heartworm preventatives are necessary evils, though you should determine how necessary based on your pet's lifestyle. There is no doubt that heartworm is a dreadful disease that threatens the lives of dogs. However, the likelihood of your dog's being bitten by an infected mosquito is slim in most places, and a mosquito-repellent (or an herbal remedy such as Wormwood or Black Walnut) is much safer for your dog and will not compromise his immune system (the way heartworm preventatives will). Should you decide to use the traditional preventative "medications," you can consider giving the pill every other or third month. Since the toxins in the pill will kill the heartworms at all stages of development, the pill would be effective in killing larvae, nymphs or adults, and it takes four months for the larvae to reach the adult stage. Thus, there is no rationale to poisoning the dog's system on a monthly basis. Lastly, do not give the pill during the winter months, since there are no mosquitoes around to pass on their infection, unless you live in a tropical environment.

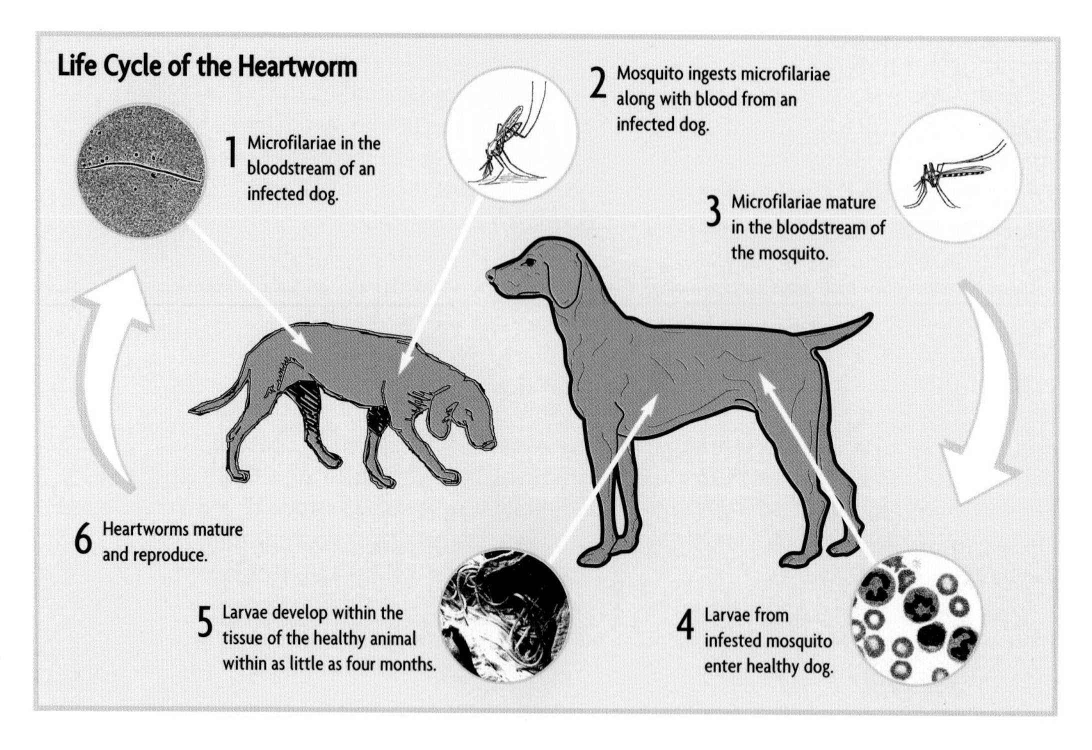

HEARTWORMS

Heartworms are thin, extended worms up to 12 inches long, which live in a dog's heart and the major blood vessels surrounding it. Dogs may have up to 200 worms. Symptoms may be loss of energy, loss of appetite, coughing, the development of a pot belly and anemia.

Heartworms are transmitted by mosquitoes. The mosquito drinks the blood of an infected dog and takes in larvae with the blood. The larvae, called microfilariae, develop within the body of the mosquito and are passed on to the next dog bitten after the larvae mature. It takes two to three weeks for the larvae to develop to the infective stage within the body of the mosquito. Dogs are usually treated at about six weeks of age and maintained on a prophylactic dose given monthly.

Blood testing for heartworms is not necessarily indicative of how seriously your dog is infected. Although this is a dangerous disease, it is not easy for a dog to be infected. Discuss the various preventatives with your vet, as there are many different types now available. Together you can decide on a safe course of prevention for your dog.

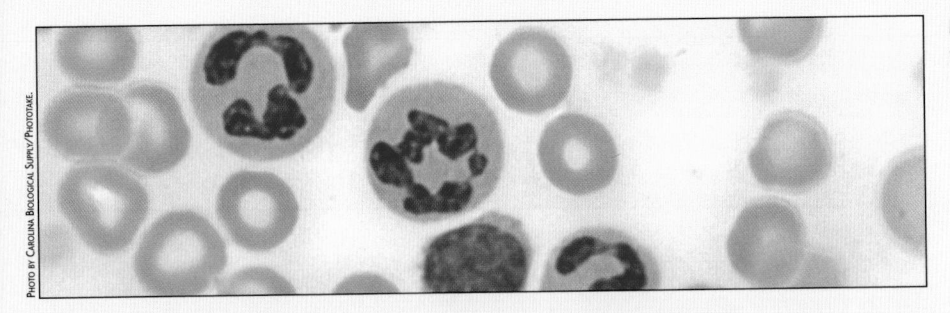

PHOTO BY CAROLINA BIOLOGICAL SUPPLY/PHOTOTAKE.

Magnified heart-worm larvae, *Dirofilaria immitis.*

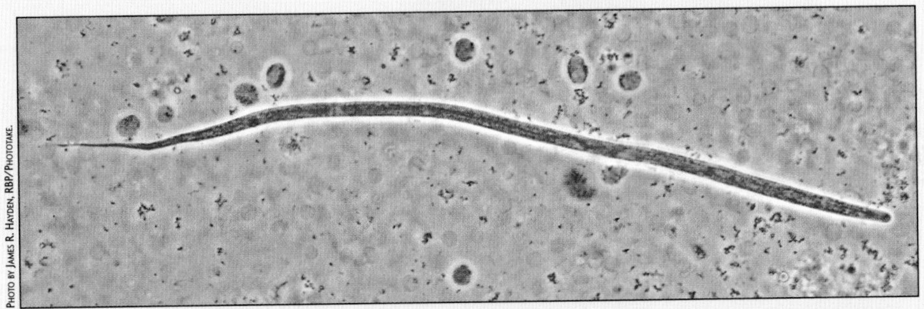

PHOTO BY JAMES R. HAYDEN, RBP/PHOTOTAKE.

Heartworm, *Dirofilaria immitis.*

PHOTO BY JAMES R. HAYDEN, RBP/PHOTOTAKE.

The heart of a dog infected with canine heart-worm, *Dirofilaria immitis.*

HOMEOPATHY:

an alternative to conventional medicine

"Less is Most"

Using this principle, the strength of a homeopathic remedy is measured by the number of serial dilutions that were undertaken to create it. The greater the number of serial dilutions, the greater the strength of the homeopathic remedy. The potency of a remedy that has been made by making a dilution of 1 part in 100 parts (or 1/100) is 1c or 1cH. If this remedy is subjected to a series of further dilutions, each one being 1/100, a more dilute and stronger remedy is produced. If the remedy is diluted in this way six times, it is called 6c or 6cH. A dilution of 6c is 1 part in 1,000,000,000,000. In general, higher potencies in more frequent doses are better for acute symptoms and lower potencies in more infrequent doses are more useful for chronic, long-standing problems.

CURING OUR DOGS NATURALLY

Holistic medicine means treating the whole animal as a unique, perfect, living being. Generally, holistic treatments do not suppress the symptoms that the body naturally produces, as do most medications prescribed by conventional doctors and vets. Holistic methods seek to cure disease by regaining balance and harmony in the patient's environment. Some of these methods include use of nutritional therapy, herbs, flower essences, aromatherapy, acupuncture, massage, chiropractic and, of course, the most popular holistic approach, homeopathy.

Homeopathy is a theory or system of treating illness with small doses of substances which, if administered in larger quantities, would produce the symptoms that the patient already has. This approach is often described as "like cures like." Although modern veterinary medicine is geared toward the "quick fix," homeopathy relies on the belief that, given the time, the body is able to heal itself and return to its natural, healthy state.

Choosing a remedy to cure a problem in our dogs is the difficult part of homeopathy. Consult with your vet for a professional diagnosis of your dog's symptoms. Often these symptoms require immediate conventional care. If your vet is willing and knowledgeable, you may attempt a homeopathic remedy. Be aware that cortisone prevents homeopathic remedies from working. There are hundreds of possibilities and combinations to cure many problems in dogs, from basic physical problems such as excessive shedding, fleas or other parasites, unattractive doggy odor, bad breath, upset tummy, obesity, dry, oily or dull coat, diarrhea, ear problems or eye discharge (including tears and dry or mucousy matter), to behavioral abnormalities such as fear of loud noises, habitual licking, poor appetite, excessive barking and various phobias. From alumina to zincum metallicum, the remedies span the planet and the imagination…from flowers and weeds to chemicals, insect droppings, diesel smoke and volcanic ash.

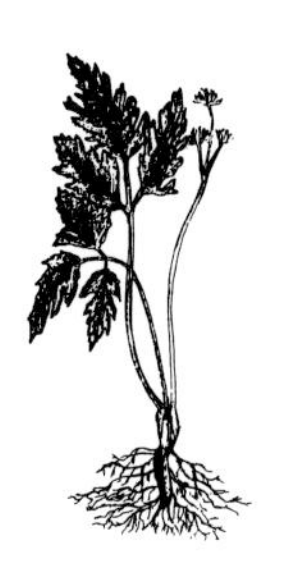

Using "Like to Treat Like"

Unlike conventional medicines that suppress symptoms, homeopathic remedies treat illnesses with small doses of substances that, if administered in larger quantities, would produce the symptoms that the patient already has. While the same homeopathic remedy can be used to treat different symptoms in different dogs, here are some interesting remedies and their uses.

Apis Mellifica
(made from honey bee venom) can be used for allergies or to reduce swelling that occurs in acutely infected kidneys.

Diesel Smoke
can be used to help control travel sickness.

Calcarea Fluorica
(made from calcium fluoride, which helps harden bone structure) can be useful in treating hard lumps in tissues.

Natrum Muriaticum
(made from common salt, sodium chloride) is useful in treating thin, thirsty dogs.

Nitricum Acidum
(made from nitric acid) is used for symptoms you would expect to see from contact with acids, such as lesions, especially where the skin joins the linings of body orifices or openings such as the lips and nostrils.

Symphytum
(made from the herb Knitbone, *Symphytum officianale*) is used to encourage bones to heal.

Urtica Urens
(made from the common stinging nettle) is used in treating painful, irritating rashes.

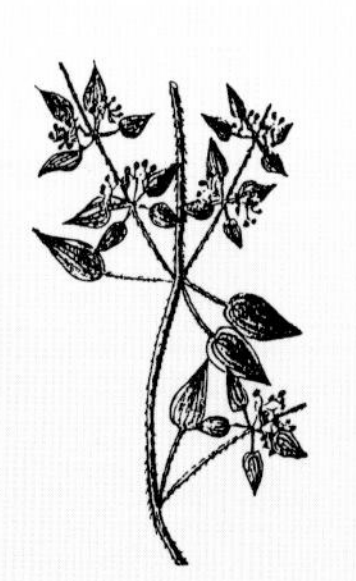

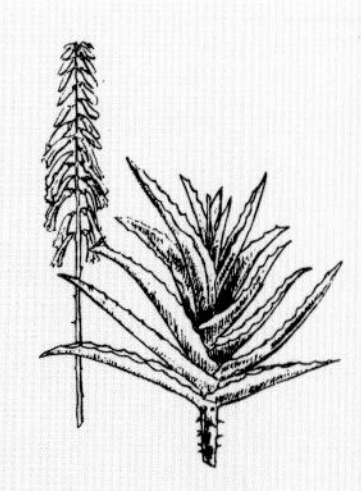

HOMEOPATHIC REMEDIES FOR YOUR DOG

Symptom/Ailment	Possible Remedy
ALLERGIES	Apis Mellifica 30c, Astacus Fluviatilis 6c, Pulsatilla 30c, Urtica Urens 6c
ALOPECIA	Alumina 30c, Lycopodium 30c, Sepia 30c, Thallium 6c
ANAL GLANDS (BLOCKED)	Hepar Sulphuris Calcareum 30c, Sanicula 6c, Silicea 6c
ARTHRITIS	Rhus Toxicodendron 6c, Bryonia Alba 6c
CATARACT	Calcarea Carbonica 6c, Conium Maculatum 6c, Phosphorus 30c, Silicea 30c
CONSTIPATION	Alumina 6c, Carbo Vegetabilis 30c, Graphites 6c, Nitricum Acidum 30c, Silicea 6c
COUGHING	Aconitum Napellus 6c, Belladonna 30c, Hyoscyamus Niger 30c, Phosphorus 30c
DIARRHEA	Arsenicum Album 30c, Aconitum Napellus 6c, Chamomilla 30c, Mercurius Corrosivus 30c
DRY EYE	Zincum Metallicum 30c
EAR PROBLEMS	Aconitum Napellus 30c, Belladonna 30c, Hepar Sulphuris 30c, Tellurium 30c, Psorinum 200c
EYE PROBLEMS	Borax 6c, Aconitum Napellus 30c, Graphites 6c, Staphysagria 6c, Thuja Occidentalis 30c
GLAUCOMA	Aconitum Napellus 30c, Apis Mellifica 6c, Phosphorus 30c
HEAT STROKE	Belladonna 30c, Gelsemium Sempervirens 30c, Sulphur 30c
HICCOUGHS	Cinchona Deficinalis 6c
HIP DYSPLASIA	Colocynthis 6c, Rhus Toxicodendron 6c, Bryonia Alba 6c
INCONTINENCE	Argentum Nitricum 6c, Causticum 30c, Conium Maculatum 30c, Pulsatilla 30c, Sepia 30c
INSECT BITES	Apis Mellifica 30c, Cantharis 30c, Hypericum Perforatum 6c, Urtica Urens 30c
ITCHING	Alumina 30c, Arsenicum Album 30c, Carbo Vegetabilis 30c, Hypericum Perforatum 6c, Mezerium 6c, Sulphur 30c
KENNEL COUGH	Drosera 6c, Ipecacuanha 30c
MASTITIS	Apis Mellifica 30c, Belladonna 30c, Urtica Urens 1m
MOTION SICKNESS	Cocculus 6c, Petroleum 6c
PATELLAR LUXATION	Gelsemium Sempervirens 6c, Rhus Toxicodendron 6c
PENIS PROBLEMS	Aconitum Napellus 30c, Hepar Sulphuris Calcareum 30c, Pulsatilla 30c, Thuja Occidentalis 6c
PUPPY TEETHING	Calcarea Carbonica 6c, Chamomilla 6c, Phytolacca 6c

Recognizing a Sick Dog

Unlike colicky babies and cranky children, our canine kids cannot tell us when they are feeling ill. Therefore, there are a number of signs that owners can identify to know that their dogs are not feeling well.

Take note for physical manifestations such as:

- unusual, bad odor, including bad breath
- excessive shedding
- wax in the ears, chronic ear irritation
- oily, flaky, dull haircoat
- mucus, tearing or similar discharge in the eyes
- fleas or mites
- mucus in stool, diarrhea
- sensitivity to petting or handling
- licking at paws, scratching face, etc.

Keep an eye out for behavioral changes as well including:

- lethargy, idleness
- lack of patience or general irritability
- lack of appetite
- phobias (fear of people, loud noises, etc.)
- strange behavior, suspicion, fear
- coprophagia
- more frequent barking
- whimpering, crying

Get Well Soon

You don't need a DVM to provide good TLC to your sick or recovering dog, but you do need to pay attention to some details that normally wouldn't bother him. The following tips will aid Fido's recovery and get him back on his paws again:

- Keep his space free of irritating smells, like heavy perfumes and air fresheners.
- Rest is the best medicine! Avoid harsh lighting that will prevent your dog from sleeping. Shade him from bright sunlight during the day and dim the lights in the evening.
- Keep the noise level down. Animals are more sensitive to sound when they are sick.
- Be attentive to any necessary temperature adjustments. A dog with a fever needs a cool room and cold liquids. A bitch that is whelping or recovering from surgery will be more comfortable in a warm room, consuming warm liquids and food.
- You wouldn't send a sick child back to school early, so don't rush your dog back into a full routine until he seems absolutely ready.

Number-One Killer Disease in Dogs: CANCER

In every age, there is a word associated with a disease or plague that causes humans to shudder. In the 21st century, that word is "cancer." Just as cancer is the leading cause of death in humans, it claims nearly half the lives of dogs that die from a natural disease as well as half the dogs that die over the age of ten years.

Described as a genetic disease, cancer becomes a greater risk as the dog ages. Vets and dog owners have become increasingly aware of the threat of cancer to dogs. Statistics reveal that one dog in every five will develop cancer, the most common of which is skin cancer. Many cancers, including prostate, ovarian and breast cancer, can be avoided by spaying and neutering our dogs by the age of six months.

Early detection of cancer can save or extend a dog's life, so it is absolutely vital for owners to have their dogs examined by a qualified vet or oncologist immediately upon detection of any abnormality. Certain dietary guidelines have also proven to reduce the onset and spread of cancer. Foods based on fish rather than beef, due to the presence of Omega-3 fatty acids, are recommended. Other amino acids such as glutamine have significant benefits for canines, particularly those breeds that show a greater susceptibility to cancer.

Cancer management and treatments promise hope for future generations of canines. Since the disease is genetic, breeders should never breed a dog whose parents, grandparents and any related siblings have developed cancer. It is difficult to know whether to exclude an otherwise healthy dog from a breeding program, as the disease does not manifest itself until the dog's senior years.

RECOGNIZE CANCER WARNING SIGNS

Since early detection can possibly rescue your dog from becoming a cancer statistic, it is essential for owners to recognize the possible signs and seek the assistance of a qualified professional.

- Abnormal bumps or lumps that continue to grow
- Bleeding or discharge from any body cavity
- Persistent stiffness or lameness
- Recurrent sores or sores that do not heal
- Inappetence
- Breathing difficulties
- Weight loss
- Bad breath or odors
- General malaise and fatigue
- Eating and swallowing problems
- Difficulty urinating and defecating

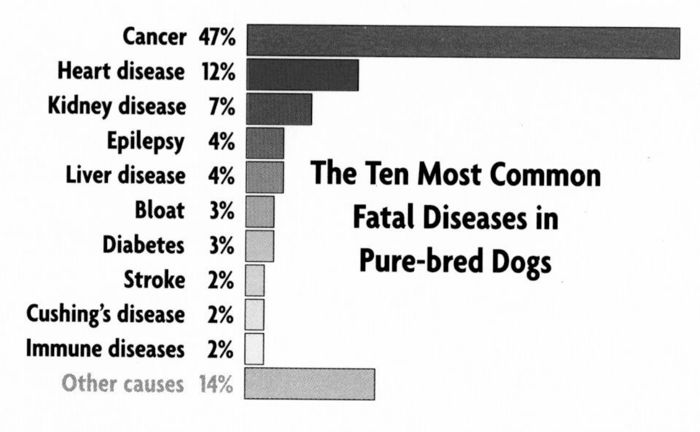

The Ten Most Common Fatal Diseases in Pure-bred Dogs

CDS: COGNITIVE DYSFUNCTION SYNDROME

"Old-Dog Syndrome"

There are many ways for you to evaluate old-dog syndrome. Veterinarians have defined CDS (cognitive dysfunction syndrome) as the gradual deterioration of cognitive abilities. These are indicated by changes in the dog's behavior. When a dog changes his routine response, and maladies have been eliminated as the cause of these behavioral changes, then CDS is the usual diagnosis.

More than half the dogs over eight years old suffer some form of CDS. The older the dog, the more chance he has of suffering from CDS. In humans, doctors often dismiss the CDS behavioral changes as part of "winding down."

There are four major signs of CDS: frequent potty accidents inside the home, sleeping much more or much less than normal, acting confused and failing to respond to social stimuli.

SYMPTOMS OF CDS

FREQUENT POTTY ACCIDENTS

- ***Urinates in the house.***
- ***Defecates in the house.***
- ***Doesn't signal that he wants to go out.***

SLEEP PATTERNS

- ***Moves much more slowly.***
- ***Sleeps more than normal during the day.***
- ***Sleeps less during the night.***

CONFUSION

- ***Goes outside and just stands there.***
- ***Appears confused with a faraway look in his eyes.***
- ***Hides more often.***
- ***Doesn't recognize friends.***
- ***Doesn't come when called.***
- ***Walks around listlessly and without a destination.***

FAILURE TO RESPOND TO SOCIAL STIMULI

- ***Comes to people less frequently, whether called or not.***
- ***Doesn't tolerate petting for more than a short time.***
- ***Doesn't come to the door when you return home.***

YOUR SENIOR TOY MANCHESTER TERRIER

The term *old* is a qualitative term. For dogs, as well as their masters, old is relative. Certainly we can all distinguish between a puppy Toy Manchester and an adult Toy Manchester—there are the obvious physical traits, such as size, appearance and facial expressions, and personality traits. Puppies and young dogs like to play with children. Children's natural exuberance is a good match for the seemingly endless energy of young dogs. They like to run, jump, chase and retrieve. When dogs grow older and cease their interaction with children, they are often thought of as being too old to play with the kids.

On the other hand, if a Toy Manchester is only exposed to people who lead quieter lifestyles, his life will normally be less active and the decrease in his activity level as he ages will not be as obvious.

If people live to be 100 years old, dogs live to be 20 years old. While this may sound like a good rule of thumb, it is very inaccurate. When trying to compare dog years to human years, you cannot make a generalization about all dogs. You can make the generalization that 14 to 16 years is a good lifespan for a Toy Manchester, which is good for any dog. Many other pure-bred dogs may only live to 8 or 9 years of age. Dogs are generally considered mature within three years, but they can reproduce even earlier. So the first three years of a dog's life are more like seven times that of comparable humans. That means a 3-year-old dog is like a 21-year-old human. As the curve of comparison shows, there is no hard and fast rule for comparing dog and human ages. The comparison is made even more difficult, for not all humans age at the same rate...and human females live longer than human males.

WHAT TO LOOK FOR IN SENIORS

Most veterinarians and behaviorists use the seven-year mark as the time to consider a dog a senior. The term *senior* does not imply that the dog is geriatric and has begun to fail in mind and body. Aging is essentially a slowing process. Humans readily admit that they feel a difference in their activity level from age 20 to 30, and then from 30 to 40, etc. By treating the seven-year-old dog as a senior, owners are able to implement certain therapeutic and preventative medical strategies with the help of their vets. A senior-care program should include at least two veterinary visits per year, screening sessions to determine the dog's health status, as well as nutritional counseling. Veterinarians determine the senior dog's health status through a blood smear for a complete blood count, serum chemistry profile with electrolytes, urinalysis, blood pressure check, electrocardiogram, ocular tonometry (pressure on the eyeball) and dental prophylaxis.

Such an extensive program for senior dogs is well advised before owners start to see the obvious physical signs of aging, such as slower and inhibited movement, graying, increased sleep/nap periods and disinterest in play and other activity. This preventative program promises a longer, healthier life for the aging dog. Among the physical problems common in aging dogs are the loss of sight and hearing, arthritis, kidney and liver failure, diabetes mellitus, heart disease and Cushing's disease (a hormonal disease).

In addition to the physical manifestations discussed, there are some behavioral changes and problems related to aging dogs. Dogs suffering from hearing or vision loss, dental discomfort or arthritis can become aggressive. Likewise, the near-deaf and/or blind dog may be startled more easily and react in an unexpectedly aggressive manner. Seniors suffering from senility can become more impatient and irritable. Housesoiling accidents are associated with loss of mobility, kidney problems and loss of sphincter control as well as plaque accumulation, physiological brain changes and reactions to medications. Older dogs, just like young puppies, can suffer from separation anxiety, which can lead to excessive barking, whining, housesoiling and destructive behavior. Seniors may become fearful of everyday sounds, such as vacuum cleaners, heaters, thunder and passing traffic. Some dogs

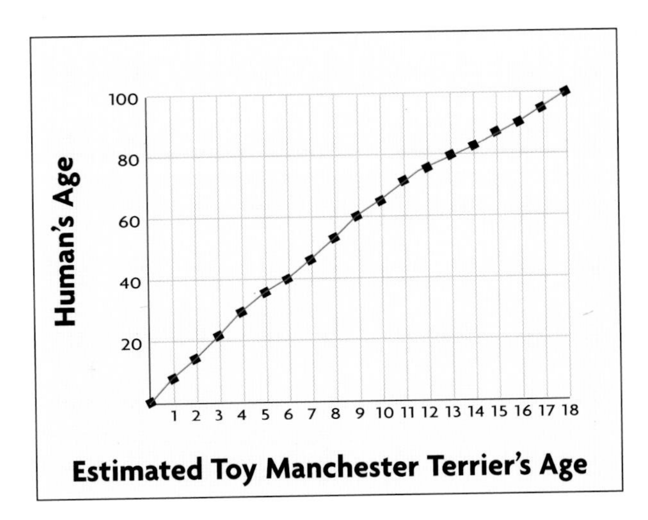

have difficulty sleeping, due to discomfort, the need for frequent toilet visits and the like.

Owners should avoid spoiling the older dog with too many treats. Obesity is a common problem in older dogs and subtracts years from their lives. Keep the senior dog as trim as possible since excess weight puts additional stress on the body's vital organs. Some breeders recommend supplementing the diet with foods high in fiber and lower in calories. Adding fresh vegetables and marrow broth to the senior's diet makes a tasty, low-calorie, low-fat supplement. Vets also offer specialty diets for senior dogs that are worth exploring.

Your dog, as he nears his twilight years, needs his owner's patience and good care more than ever. Never punish an older dog for an accident or abnormal behavior. For all the years of love, protection and companionship that your dog has provided, he deserves special attention and courtesies. The older dog may need to relieve himself at 3 a.m. because he can no longer hold it for eight hours. Older dogs may not be able to remain crated for more than two or three hours. It may be time to give up a sofa or chair to your old friend. Although he may not seem as enthusiastic about your attention and petting, he does appreciate the considerations you offer as he gets older.

Your Toy Manchester does not understand why his world is slowing down. Owners must make their dogs' transition into the golden years as pleasant and rewarding as possible.

WHEN THE TIME COMES

You are never fully prepared to make a rational decision about putting your dog to sleep. It is very obvious that you love your Toy Manchester or you would not be reading this book. Putting a loved dog to sleep is extremely difficult. It is a decision that must be made with your veterinarian. You are usually forced to make the decision when your dog experiences one or more life-threatening symptoms, requiring you to seek veterinary help.

If the prognosis of the malady indicates the end is near and your beloved pet will only suffer more and experience no enjoyment for the balance of his life, then euthanasia is the right choice.

WHAT IS EUTHANASIA?

Euthanasia derives from the Greek, meaning *good death*. In other words, it means the planned, painless killing of a dog suffering from a painful, incurable condition, or who is so aged that he cannot walk, see, eat or control his excretory functions.

Euthanasia is usually accomplished by injection with an overdose of an anesthesia or barbiturate. Aside from the prick of the needle, the experience is usually painless.

Making the Decision

The decision to euthanize your dog is never easy. The days during which the dog becomes ill and the end occurs can be unusually stressful for you. If this is your first experience with the death of a loved one, you may need the comfort dictated by your religious beliefs. If you are the head of the family and have children, you should have involved them in the decision of putting your Toy Manchester to sleep. Usually your dog can be maintained on drugs at the vet's clinic for a few days in order to give you ample time to make a decision. During this time, talking with members of your family or even people who have lived through this same experience can ease the burden of your inevitable decision.

The Final Resting Place

Dogs can have some of the same privileges as humans. The remains of your beloved dog can be buried in a pet cemetery, which is generally expensive. Dogs who have died at home can be buried in your yard in a place suitably marked with a stone or a newly planted tree or bush. Alternatively, dogs can be cremated individually and the ashes returned to you. A less expensive option is mass cremation, although, of course, the ashes of your individual dog cannot then be returned. Vets can usually arrange the cremation on your behalf or help you locate a pet cemetery. The cost of these options should always be discussed frankly and openly with your vet.

Getting Another Dog?

The grief of losing your beloved dog will be as lasting as the grief of losing a human friend or relative. In most cases, if your dog died of old age (if there is such a thing), he had slowed down considerably. Do you want a new Toy Manchester puppy to replace him? Or are you better off finding a more mature Toy Manchester, say two to three years of age, which will usually be house-trained and will have an already developed personality. In this case, you can find out if you like each other after a few hours of being together.

The decision is, of course, your own. Do you want another Toy Manchester or perhaps a different breed so as to avoid comparison with your beloved friend? Most people usually stay with the same breed because they know and love the characteristics of that breed. Then, too, they often know people who have the same breed and perhaps they are lucky enough that a breeder they know and respect expects a litter soon.

SHOWING YOUR

TOY MANCHESTER TERRIER

When you purchase your Toy Manchester, you will make it clear to the breeder whether you want one just as a lovable companion and pet, or if you hope to be buying a Toy Manchester with show prospects. No reputable breeder will sell you a young puppy and tell you that it is *definitely* of show quality, for so much can go wrong during the early months of a puppy's development. If you plan to show, what you will hopefully have acquired is a puppy with "show potential."

To the novice, exhibiting a Toy Manchester in the show ring may look easy, but it takes a lot of hard work and devotion to do top winning at a show such as the prestigious Westminster Kennel Club dog show, not to mention a little luck too!

The first concept that the canine novice learns when watching a dog show is that each dog first competes against members of his own breed. Once the judge has selected the best member of each breed (Best of Breed), provided that the show is judged on a Group system, that chosen dog will compete with other dogs in his group. Finally, the dogs chosen first in each group will compete for Best in Show.

The second concept that you must understand is that the dogs are not actually compared against one another. The judge compares each dog against its breed standard, the written description of the ideal specimen that is approved by the American Kennel Club (AKC). While some early breed standards were indeed based on specific dogs that were famous or popular, many dedicated enthusiasts say that a perfect specimen, as described in the standard, has never walked into a show ring, has never been bred and, to the woe of dog breeders around the globe, does not exist. Breeders attempt to get as close to this ideal as possible with every litter, but theoretically the "perfect" dog is so elusive that it is impossible. (And if the "perfect" dog were born, breeders and judges would never agree that it was indeed "perfect.")

If you are interested in exploring the world of dog showing, your best bet is to join your local breed club or the national parent club, which is the American Manchester Terrier Club. These clubs often host both regional and national specialties, shows only for Manchesters, which can include conformation as well as obedience and agility trials. Even if you have no intention of competing with your Toy Manchester Terrier, a specialty is like a festival for lovers of the breed who congregate to share their favorite topic: Toy Manchester Terriers! Clubs also send out newsletters, and some organize training days and seminars in order that people may learn more about their chosen breed. To locate the breed club closest to you, contact the AKC, which furnishes the rules and regulations for all of these events plus general dog registration and other basic requirements of dog ownership.

The AKC offers three kinds of conformation shows: an all-breed show (for all recognized breeds), a specialty show (for one breed only, usually sponsored by the parent club) and a Group show (for all breeds in the group).

Dog showing does not offer "co-ed" classes. Dogs and bitches never compete against each other in the classes. Non-champion dogs are called "class dogs" because they compete in one of five classes. Dogs are entered in a particular class depending on age and previous show wins. To begin, there is the Puppy Class (for 6- to 9-month-olds and for 9- to 12-month-olds); this class is followed by the Novice Class (for dogs that have not won any first prizes except in the Puppy Class or three first prizes in the Novice Class and have not accumulated any points toward their champion title); the Bred-by-Exhibitor Class (for dogs handled by their breeders or handled by one of the breeder's immediate family); the American-bred Class (for dogs bred in the US); and the Open Class (for any dog that is not a champion).

Toy Manchesters are natural showmen and many excel in the show ring. Exhibiting your Toy Manchester may be the perfect hobby sport for you and your dog.

The judge at the show begins judging the Puppy Class, first dogs and then bitches, and proceeds through the classes. The judge places his winners first through fourth in each class. In the

Winners Class, the first-place winners of each class compete with one another to determine Winners Dog and Winners Bitch. The judge also places a Reserve Winners Dog and Reserve Winners Bitch, which could be awarded the points in the case of a disqualification. The Winners Dog and Winners Bitch, the two that are awarded the points for the breed, then compete with any champions of record entered in the show, which are usually called "specials." The judge reviews the Winners Dog, Winners Bitch and all of the champions to select his Best of Breed. The Best of Winners is selected between the Winners Dog and Winners Bitch. Were one of these two to be selected Best of Breed, he or she would automatically be named Best of Winners as well. Finally the judge selects his Best of Opposite Sex to the Best of Breed winner.

At a Group show or all-breed show, the Best of Breed winners from each breed then compete against one another for Group One through Group Four. The judge compares each Best of Breed to his breed standard, and the dog that most closely lives up to the ideal for his breed is selected as Group One. Finally, all seven group winners (from the Toy Group, Hound Group, Working Group, etc.) compete for Best in Show.

To find out about dog shows in your area, you can subscribe to the American Kennel Club's monthly magazine, the *American Kennel Gazette* and the accompanying *Events Calendar*. You can also look in your local newspaper for advertisements for dog shows in your area or go on the Internet to the AKC's website, www.akc.org.

If your Toy Manchester is six months of age or older and registered with the AKC, you can enter him in a dog show where the breed is offered classes. Provided that your Toy Manchester does not have a disqualifying fault, he can compete. Only unaltered dogs can be entered in a dog show, so if you have spayed or neutered your Toy Manchester, your dog cannot compete in conformation shows. The reason for this is simple. Dog shows are the main forum to prove which representatives of a breed are worthy of being bred. Only dogs that have achieved championships—the AKC "seal of approval" for quality in pure-bred dogs—should be bred. Altered dogs, however, can participate in other AKC events such as obedience trials and the Canine Good Citizen program.

OBEDIENCE TRIALS

Obedience trials in the US trace back to the early 1930s when organized obedience training was developed to demonstrate how well dog and owner could work

CLUB CONTACTS

You can get information about dog shows from the national kennel clubs:

American Kennel Club
5580 Centerview Dr., Raleigh, NC 27606-3390
www.akc.org

United Kennel Club
100 E. Kilgore Road, Kalamazoo, MI 49002
www.ukcdogs.com

Canadian Kennel Club
89 Skyway Ave., Suite 100, Etobicoke, Ontario
M9W 6R4 Canada
www.ckc.ca

The Kennel Club
1-5 Clarges St., Piccadilly,
London W1Y 8AB, UK
www.the-kennel-club.org.uk

together. The pioneer of obedience trials is Mrs. Helen Whitehouse Walker, a Standard Poodle fancier, who designed a series of exercises after the Associated Sheep, Police Army Dog Society of Great Britain. Since the days of Mrs. Walker, obedience trials have grown by leaps and bounds, and today there are over 2,000 trials held in the US every year, with more than 100,000 dogs competing. Any registered AKC dog can enter an obedience trial, regardless of conformational disqualifications or neutering.

Obedience trials are divided into three levels of progressive difficulty. At the first level, the Novice, dogs compete for the title Companion Dog (CD); at the intermediate level, the Open, dogs compete for the title Companion Dog Excellent (CDX); and at the advanced level, the Utility, dogs compete for the title Utility Dog (UD). Classes are sub-divided into "A" (for beginners) and "B" (for more experienced handlers). A perfect score at any level is 200, and a dog must score 170 or better to earn a "leg," of which three are needed to earn the title. To earn points, the dog must score more than 50% of the available points in each exercise; the possible points range from 20 to 40.

Once a dog has earned the UD title, he can compete with other proven obedience dogs for the coveted title of Utility Dog Excellent (UDX), which requires that the dog win "legs" in ten shows. Utility Dogs who earn "legs" in Open B and Utility B earn points toward their Obedience Trial Champion title. In 1977, the title Obedience Trial Champion (OTCh.) was established by the AKC. To become an OTCh., a dog needs to earn 100 points, which requires three first places in Open B and Utility under three different judges.

AGILITY TRIALS

Having had its origins in the UK back in 1977, AKC agility had its official beginning in the US in August 1994, when the first licensed agility trials were held.

The AKC allows all registered breeds (including Miscellaneous Class breeds) to participate, providing the dog is 12 months of age or older. Agility is designed so that the handler demonstrates how well the dog can work at his side. The handler directs his dog over an obstacle course that includes jumps as well as tires, the dog walk, weave poles, pipe tunnels, collapsed tunnels, etc. While working his way through the course, the dog must keep one eye and ear on the handler and the rest of his body on the course. The handler gives verbal and hand signals to guide the dog through the course.

Agility is great fun for dog and owner with many rewards for everyone involved. Interested owners should join a training club that has obstacles and experienced agility handlers who can introduce you and your dog to the "ropes" (and tires, tunnels, etc.).

TRACKING

Any dog is capable of tracking, using his nose to follow a trail. Tracking tests are exciting and competitive ways to test your Toy Manchester Terrier's ability. The AKC started tracking tests in 1937, when the first AKC-licensed test took place as part of the Utility level at an obedience trial. Ten years later in 1947, the AKC offered the first title, Tracking Dog (TD). It was not until 1980 that the AKC added the Tracking Dog Excellent title (TDX), which was followed by the Versatile Surface Tracking title (VST) in 1995. The title Champion Tracker (CT) is awarded to a dog who has earned all three titles.

In the beginning level of tracking, the owner follows the dog through a field on a long lead. To earn the TD title, the dog must follow a track laid by a human 30 to 120 minutes prior. The track is about 500 yards with up to 5 directional changes. The TDX requires that the dog follow a track that is 3 to 5 hours old over a course up to 1,000 yards with up to 7 directional changes. The VST requires that the dog follow a track up to 5 hours old through an urban setting.

EARTHDOG TESTS

All of the terriers as well as the Dachshund can participate in earthdog tests. These events are designed to test a dog's ability to chase and pursue quarry, making use of live rats (thankfully caged) or artificial lures. Dogs are required to work the quarry (barking, digging and scratching shows the level of the dog's interest in the quarry) as well as find and follow a scent down into an earthen tunnel. Depending on the level of competition, dogs can earn the titles: Junior Earthdog (JE), Senior Earthdog (SE) and Master Earthdog (ME).

AMERICAN KENNEL CLUB TITLES

The AKC offers over 40 different titles to dogs in competition. Depending on the events that your dog can enter, different titles apply. Some titles can be applied as prefixes, meaning that they are placed before the dog's name (e.g., Ch. King of the Road) and others are used as suffixes, placed after the dog's name (e.g., King of the Road, CD).

These titles are used as prefixes:

Conformation Dog Shows
- Ch. (Champion)

Obedience Trials
- NOC (National Obedience Champion)
- OTCH (Obedience Trial Champion)
- VCCH (Versatile Companion Champion)

Tracking Tests
- CT [Champion Tracker (TD,TDX and VST)]

Agility Trials
- MACH (Master Agility Champion)
- MACH2, MACH3, MACH4, etc. .

Field Trials
- FC (Field Champion)
- AFC (Amateur Field Champion)
- NFC (National Field Champion)
- NAFC (National Amateur Field Champion)
- NOGDC (National Open Gun Dog Champion)
- AKC GDSC (AKC Gun Dog Stake Champion)
- AKC RGDSC (AKC Retrieving Gun Dog Stake Champion)

Herding Trials
- HC (Herding Champion)

Dual
- DC (Dual Champion — Ch. and FC)

Triple
- TC (Triple Champion — Ch., FC and OTCH)

Coonhounds
- NCH (Nite Champion)
- GNCH (Grand Nite Champion)
- SHNCH (Senior Grand Nite Champion)
- GCH (Senior Champion)
- SGCH (Senior Grand Champion)
- GFC (Grand Field Champion)
- SGFC (Senior Grand Field Champion)
- WCH (Water Race Champion)
- GWCH (Water Race Grand Champion)
- SGWCH (Senior Grand Water Race Champion)

These titles are used as suffixes:

Obedience
- CD (Companion Dog)
- CDX (Companion Dog Excellent)
- UD (Utility Dog)
- UDX (Utility Dog Excellent)
- VCD1 (Versatile Companion Dog 1)
- VCD2 (Versatile Companion Dog 2)
- VCD3 (Versatile Companion Dog 3)
- VCD4 (Versatile Companion Dog 4)

Tracking Tests
- TD (Tracking Dog)
- TDX (Tracking Dog Excellent)
- VST (Variable Surface Tracker)

Agility Trials
- NA (Novice Agility)
- OA (Open Agility)
- AX (Agility Excellent)
- MX (Master Agility Excellent)
- NAJ (Novice Jumpers with weaves)
- OAJ (Open Jumpers with weaves)
- AXJ (Excellent Jumpers with weaves)
- MXJ (Master Excellent Jumpers with weaves)

Hunting Test
- JH (Junior Hunter)
- SH (Senior Hunter)
- MH (Master Hunter)

Herding Test
- HT (Herding Tested)
- PT (Pre-Trial Tested)
- HS (Herding Started)
- HI (Herding Intermediate)
- HX (Herding Excellent)

Lure Coursing
- JC (Junior Courser)
- SC (Senior Courser)
- MC (Master Courser)

Earthdog
- JE (Junior Earthdog)
- SE (Senior Earthdog)
- ME (Master Earthdog)

Lure Coursing
- JC (Junior Courser)
- SC (Senior Courser)
- MC (Master Courser)

BEHAVIOR OF YOUR TOY MANCHESTER TERRIER

As a Toy Manchester owner, you have selected your dog so that you and your loved ones can have a companion, a protector, a friend and a four-legged family member. You invest time, money and effort to care for and train the family's new charge. Of course, this chosen canine behaves perfectly! Well, perfectly like a *dog*.

THINK LIKE A DOG

Dogs do not think like humans, nor do humans think like dogs, though we try. Unfortunately, a dog is incapable of comprehending how humans think, so the responsibility falls on the owner to adopt a viable canine mindset. Dogs cannot rationalize, and dogs exist in the present moment. Many a dog owner makes the mistake in training of thinking that he can reprimand his dog for something the dog did a while ago. Basically, you cannot even reprimand a dog for something he did 20 seconds ago! Either catch him in the act or forget it! It is a waste of your and your dog's time—in his mind, you are reprimanding him for whatever he is doing at that moment.

The following behavioral problems represent some which owners most commonly encounter. Every dog is unique and every situation is unique. No author could purport for you to solve your Toy Manchester's problems simply by reading a chapter. Here we outline some basic "dogspeak" so that owners" chances of solving behavioral problems are increased. Discuss bad habits with your veterinarian and he/she can recommend a behavioral specialist to consult in appropriate cases. Since behavioral abnormalities are the main reason that owners abandon their pets, we hope that you will make a valiant effort to solve your Toy Manchester's problems. Patience and understanding are virtues that must dwell in every pet-loving household.

SEPARATION ANXIETY

Your Toy Manchester may howl, whine or otherwise vocalize his displeasure at your leaving the house and his being left alone. This is a normal reaction, no different from the child who cries as his mother leaves him on the first day at school. In fact, constant attention can lead to separation anxiety in the first place. If you are constantly making a fuss of your dog, he will come to expect this from you all of the time and it will be more traumatic for him when you are not there. Obviously, you enjoy spending time with your dog, and he thrives on your love and attention. However, it should not become a dependent relationship where he is heartbroken without you.

One thing you can do to minimize separation anxiety is to make your entrances and exits as low-key as possible. Do not give your dog a long drawn-out good-bye, and do not overly lavish him with hugs and kisses when you return. This is giving in to the attention that he craves, and it will only make him miss it more when you are away. Another thing you can try is to give your dog a treat when you leave; this will not only keep him occupied and keep his mind off the fact that you have just left, but it will also help him associate your leaving with a pleasant experience.

When the dog is alone in the house, he should be confined to his designated dog-proof area of the house. This should be the area in which he sleeps and already feels comfortable, so he will feel more at ease when he is alone.

"LONELY WOLF"

The number of dogs that suffer from separation anxiety is on the rise as more and more pet owners find themselves at work all day. New attention is being paid to this problem, which is especially hard to diagnose since it is only evident when the dog is alone. Research is currently being done to help educate dog owners about separation anxiety and how they can help minimize this problem in their dogs.

BARKING

Admittedly, the Toy Manchester has more to say than many other dogs, given his superior intelligence and superb way of voicing his concerns. Indeed, barking is a dog's way of "talking." It can be somewhat frustrating because it is not always easy to tell what a dog means by his bark—is he excited, happy, frightened or angry? Whatever it is that the dog is trying to say, he should not be punished for barking. It is only when the barking becomes excessive, and when the excessive barking becomes a bad habit, that the behavior needs to be modified.

Fortunately, Toy Manchesters, making excellent alarm dogs, but in general can be more "barky" than many other dogs. Barking is not always an undesirable behavior; in fact, it is often a commendable one. If an intruder came into your home in the middle of the night and your Toy Manchester barked a warning, wouldn't you be pleased? You would probably deem your dog a hero, a wonderful guardian and protector of the home. On the other hand, if a friend drops by unexpectedly and rings the doorbell and is greeted with a sudden sharp bark, you would probably be annoyed at the dog. But in reality, isn't this just the same behavior? The dog does not know any better...unless he sees who is at the door and it is someone he knows, he will bark as a means of vocalizing that his (and your) territory is being threatened. While your friend is not posing a threat, it is all the same to the dog. Barking is his means of letting you know that there is an intrusion, whether friend or foe, on your property. This type of barking is instinctive and should not be discouraged.

Excessive habitual barking, however, is a problem that should be corrected early on. As your Toy Manchester grows up, you will be able to tell when his barking is purposeful and when it is for no reason. You will become able to distinguish your dog's different barks and their meanings. For example, the bark when someone comes to the door will be different from the bark when he is excited to see you. It is similar to a person's tone of voice, except that the dog has to rely totally on tone of voice because he does not have the benefit of using words. An incessant barker will be evident at an early age.

There are some things that encourage a dog to bark. For example, if your dog barks nonstop for a few minutes and you give him a treat to quiet him, he believes that you are rewarding him for barking. He will associate barking with getting a treat, and will keep doing it until he is rewarded.

AGGRESSION

Toy Manchesters are not known to be aggressive toward people or other dogs, though this is a problem that should concern all responsible dog owners. Aggression can be a very big problem in dogs; although it is more common in breeds with fighting backgrounds, it can occur in dogs or any breed. Aggression, when not controlled, always becomes dangerous. An aggressive dog, no matter the size, may lunge at, bite or even attack a person or another dog. Aggressive behavior is not to be tolerated. It is more than just inappropriate behavior; it is not safe, and even small dogs can inflict damage. It is painful for a family to watch their dog become unpredictable in his behavior to the point where they are afraid of him. While not all aggressive behavior is dangerous, growling, baring teeth, etc., can be frightening. It is important to ascertain why the dog is acting in this manner. Aggression is a display of dominance, and the dog should not have the dominant role in its pack, which is, in this case, your family.

The best solution is to consult a behavioral specialist, one who has experience with the Toy Manchester or similar breeds if possible. Together, perhaps you can pinpoint the cause of your dog's aggression and do something about it. An aggressive dog cannot be trusted, and a dog that cannot be trusted is not safe to have as a family pet. If, very unusually, you find that your pet has become untrustworthy and you feel it necessary to seek a new home with a more suitable family and environment, explain fully to the new owners all your reasons for rehoming the dog to be fair to all concerned.

IT'S PLAY TIME

Physical games like pulling contests, wrestling, jumping and teasing should not be encouraged. Inciting a dog's crazy behavior tends to confuse him. The owner has to be able to control his dog at all times. Even in play, your dog has to know that you are the leader and that you decide when to play and when to behave calmly.

DIGGING

Digging, which is seen as a destructive behavior to humans, is actually quite a natural behavior in dogs. Terriers (the earthdogs) are most associated with digging, and you may be amazed at how talented yor Toy Manchester is with his paws! Any dog's desire to dig can be irrepressible and most frustrating to his owners. When digging occurs in your yard, it is actually a normal behavior redirected into something the dog can do in his everyday life. In the wild, a dog would be actively seeking food, making his own shelter, etc. He would be using his paws in a purposeful manner for his survival. Since you provide him with food and shelter, he has no need to use his paws for these purposes, and so the energy that he would be using may manifest itself in the form of little holes all over your yard and flower beds.

Perhaps your dog is digging as a reaction to boredom—it is somewhat similar to someone eating a whole bag of chips in front of the TV—because they are there and there is nothing better to do! Basically, the answer is to provide the dog with adequate play and exercise so that his mind and paws are occupied, and so that he feels as if he is doing something useful.

Of course, digging is easiest to control if it is stopped as soon as possible, but it is often hard to catch a dog in the act. If your dog is a compulsive digger and is not easily distracted by other activities, you can designate an area on your property where he is allowed to dig. If you catch him digging in an off-limits area of the yard, immediately bring him to the approved area and praise him for digging there. Keep a close eye on him so that you can catch him in the act—that is the only way to make him understand what is permitted and what is not. If you take him to a hole he dug an hour ago and tell him "No," he will understand that you are not fond of holes, dirt or flowers. If you catch him while he is stifle-deep in your tulips, that is when he will get your message.

CHEWING

The national canine pastime is chewing! Every dog loves to sink his "canines" into a tasty bone, but if a bone is not available, almost anything will do. Dogs need to chew, to massage their gums, to make their new teeth feel better and to exercise their jaws. This is a natural behavior deeply embedded in all things canine. Our role as owners is not to stop the dog's chewing, but to redirect it to positive, chew-worthy objects. Be an informed owner and purchase proper chew toys like strong nylon bones that will not splinter. Be sure that the objects are safe and durable, since your dog's safety is at risk. Again, the owner is responsible for ensuring a dog-proof environment. The best answer is prevention, that is, put your shoes, handbags and other tasty objects in their proper places (out of the reach of the growing canine mouth). Direct your puppy to his toys whenever you see him tasting the furniture legs or the leg of your pants. Make a loud noise to attract the pup's attention and immediately escort him to his chew toy and engage him with the toy for at least four minutes, praising and encouraging him all the while.

Some trainers recommend deterrents, such as hot pepper, a bitter spice or a product designed for this purpose, to discourage the dog from chewing unwanted objects. Test these products yourself before investing in large quantities.

JUMPING UP

Jumping up is a dog's friendly way of saying hello! Some dog owners do not mind when their dog jumps up. The problem arises when guests come to the house and the dog greets them in the same manner—whether they like it or not! However friendly the greeting may be, chances are that your visitors will not appreciate your dog's enthusiasm. The dog will not be able to distinguish upon whom he can jump and whom he cannot. Therefore, it is probably best to discourage this behavior entirely.

Pick a command such as "Off" (avoid using "Down" since you will use that for the dog to lie down) and tell him "Off" when he

Most Toy Manchester Terriers lead problem-free existences and do not exhibit any unusual behavior problems. A well-informed owner will enjoy a mostly stress-free life with his dog.

jumps up. Place him on the ground on all fours and have him sit, praising him the whole time. Always lavish him with praise and petting when he is in the sit position. In this way you can give him a warm affectionate greeting, let him know that you are as excited to see him as he is to see you and instill good manners at the same time!

FOOD STEALING

Is your dog devising ways of stealing food from your coffee table? If so, you must answer the following questions: Is your Toy Manchester hungry, or is he "constantly famished" like many dogs seem to be? Face it, some dogs are more food-motivated than others. They are totally obsessed by the smell of food and can only think of their next meal. Food stealing is terrific fun and always yields a great reward—*food*, glorious food.

The owner's goal, therefore, is to be sensible about where food is placed in the home, and to reprimand your dog whenever he is caught in the act of stealing. But remember, only reprimand your dog if you actually see him stealing, not later when the crime is discovered, for that will be of no use at all and will only serve to confuse him.

BEGGING

Just like food stealing, begging is a favorite pastime of hungry puppies! It achieves that same terrific result—*food*! Dogs quickly learn that their owners keep the "good food" for themselves, and that we humans do not dine on dry food alone. Begging is a conditioned response related to a specific stimulus, time and place. The sounds of the kitchen, cans and bottles opening, crinkling bags, the smell of food in preparation, etc., will excite the dog and soon the paws are in the air!

Here is the solution to stopping this behavior: Never give in to a beggar! You are rewarding the dog for sitting pretty, jumping up, whining and rubbing his nose into you by giving him food. By ignoring the dog, you will (eventually) force the behavior into extinction. Note that the behavior is likely to get worse before it disappears, so be sure there are not any "softies" in the family who will give in to little "Oliver" every time he whimpers, "More, please."

INDEX

*Page numbers in **boldface** indicate illustrations.*

Adult diets 69
Age 90
Aggression 23, 152
—fear 87
Agility 22, 107, 147, 148
AKC 26, , 147
All-breed show 146
American dog tick 124
American Kennel Club 18, 26, 144
—address 147
—breed standard 27
American Kennel Gazette 146
American Manchester Terrier Club 18, 145
American-bred Class 145
Ancylostoma braziliense 129
Ancylostoma caninum **129**
Ancylostoma tubaeforme *129*
Ascaris lumbricoides **128**
Australian Terrier 10
Auto-immune skin conditions 118
Axelrod, Dr. Herbert R. 127
Barking 22, 24, 151
Bathing 74
Bedding 45
Begging 155
Behavior 153
—destructive 154
—problems 150
Bell Boy 19
Best of Breed 144, 146
Best of Opposite Sex 146
Black and Tan Terrier 9-10, 16
Boarding 81
Bones 46, 154
Boredom 153
Bowls 48
Bred-by-Exhibitor Class 145
Breed name 18
Breed standard 26, 144
Breeder 54
—finding a 34
British Manchester Terrier Club 16
Brown dog tick **127**
Burial 143
Caius, Dr. Johannes 13
Campbell Kennels 18
Canada 12, 19
Canadian Kennel Club 19
—address 147
Canadian Manchester Terrier Club 19
Cancer 138
Canine cough 113, 114-115
Canine development schedule 90
Cat 98
Cawdor kennels 18
CDS 139
Champion Tracker 148
Chew toys 154
Chewing 22, 66, 93, 154
Cheyletiellosis 126
Children 22, 104
Chocolate 60
Christie, Agatha 15
Clark, R.D. 18
Coat 22, 23
Cognitive Dysfunction Syndrome 139
Cold weather 22
Collar 48, 98
Colostrum 68
Come 103
Commands 99, 100-105
Companion Dog 21, 147
Companion Dog Excellent 147
Control 89
Coronavirus 113, 115
Crate 22, 42, 58, 64, 79, 92, 94
—training 58, 94
Crying 64
Ctenocephalides **122**
Ctenocephalides canis **120**
Dachshund 10
Deer tick **125**
Demodex mites 125
Dempsey Kennels 19
Dempsey's Tippy Tin 19
Dempsey, Mrs. Dixie 19
Dental care 77, 113
Dental health 77
Dermacentor variabilis **124-125**
Dermanyssus gallinae 127
Destructive behavior 141, 154
Deutscher Jagdterrier 10
Development of the breed 10
Diet 67
—adult 69
—change in 73
—puppy 68
—senior 69
Digging 153
Dipylidium caninum **130**
Dirofilaria immitis **133**
Discipline 97
Distemper 113, 115
Doberman Pinscher 10
Dog shows 26
Down 100
Dusky kennels 19
Ear cropping 15
Ear-mite 127
Earthdog tests 148
Echinococcus multilocularis **130**
England 9, 12-16
English Toy Terrier 16, 18
Europe 12
Euthanasia 142
Eutrombicula alfreddugesi 127
Evan's Clipper 18
Events Calendar 146
Exercise 22
External parasites 120-127
Family dog 21
Family introduction to pup 54
Fear period 60
Fence 52
Flea **120**, 121, **122-123**, 124, 130
—life cycle 121-122, **123**
Food 67
—allergy 118
—intolerance 118
—stealing 155
—storage 67
—treats 106
Gender 37
German Hunting Terrier 10
Gesner 14
Gilmore's Garden Westminster Show 18
Golden Embkem of Hartford 16
Golden Ermine of Harford 16
Greene, Mrs. 16
Grooming 22, 73
Group show 145-146
Harford Kennels 16
Harvester Lassie 18
Health concerns 23
Heartworm 113, **131-133**
—life cycle **132**
—preventatives 131
Heel 104
Hepatitis 113, 115
Hip dysplasia 113
Holistic medicine 134-136
Hookworm **129**
House-training 22, 88-97
Housebreaking 22, 88-97
Housing 89
Hulme, Mr. John 10, 12
Identification 79, 82-83
Insect Growth Regulator 122, 124
Intelligence 22
Internal parasites 127-133
Italian Greyhound 10
Johnny Zero of Kent 19
Judge 26, 145
Jumping up 154

Junior Earthdog 148
Kay Ess Kennels 19
Kennel Club, The 15
—address 147
—registers 18
—stud book 15
Kricket of Kent 18
Lady Blondin 19
Lancashire Heeler 10
Lap dogs 25
Leash 47, 98
Leggs-Calves-Perthes 24
Leptospirosis 113, 115
Lever 18
Lice **126**
Life expectancy 140, **141**
Lifespan 22, 24, 140
Little, G. Calder 18
Louisiana Squirrel Dog 12
Lupus 118
Manchester Terrier Club of America 18
Mange mite **126**
Master Earthdog 148
Milk 68
Miniature Black and Tans 16
Mite **125**
Moscow Toy Terrier 10
Mulch 60
Nail care 77
Napoleon-complex-suffering toy dogs 23
Neutering 115, 113
Nipping 62
Novice Class 145
Nutrition 68
Obedience 22
—class 84, 106
Obedience Trial Champion 147
Obedience Trial Champion title 147
Obedience trials 146-147
Obesity 142
Off 154
Old dog syndrome 139
Old English Terrier 9
Open Class 145
Origin of the breed 9-10
Otodectes cynotis 127
Outdoor training 88
Owens, Mrs. Ruby 18-19
Owner suitability 21-23
Parainfluenza 113
Parasite
—bites 117
—external 120-127
—internal 127-133
Parvovirus 113, 115
Personality 21-23
Philadelphia Grand National Dog Show 16
Police Army Dog Society of Great Britain 147
Pollen allergy 118
Popularity 21
Positive reinforcement 22
Preventative medicine 111
Psoroptes bovis **126**
Punishment 98
Puppy
—appearance 38
—financial responsibility 46
—first trip to the vet 53
—food 68
—health 114
—home preparation 41
—ownership 37
—problems 60, 62
—selection 34, 36
—socialization 60
—training 65
Puppy Class 145
Puppy-proofing 51
Rabies 113, 115
Ratters 9
Ratting contests 12-13
Recognition of breed in England 18
Reiman, A.H. 19
Reserve Winners Bitch 146
Reserve Winners Dog 146
Rhabditis **128**
Rhipicephalus sanguineus **127**
Roosevelt, President Teddy 15
Roundworm **128**
Russell kennels 18
Russell's Sport of Harford 19
Safety 22
Sarcoptes mite 126
Schmidt, Mrs. G. Campbell 18
Senior 140
—diet 69
Senior Earthdog 148
Sensitivity to injections 111
Separation anxiety 64, 141, 150
Show potential 144
Showing 144
Sit 100
Skin care 23
Skin problems 116
—inherited 117
Socialization 64
Spaying 115
Specialty show 145
Standard 26, 144
Standard variety 10, 16, 18
Stay 101
Stealing food 155
Strongyloides 131
Tapeworm 130
Temperament 21-23
Thebromine 60
Thompson, H. T. 18
Thorndike's Theory of Learning 97
Thorndike, Dr. Edward 97
Threadworm 131
Thyroid problems 24-25
Tick **124-125**
Tiny 12, 19
Tony's Zkay 19
Toxocara canis 128
Toy Black and Tan 18
Toy Terriers 18
Toy variety 10
Toys 45, 53, 154
Tracheobronchitis 114
Tracking 148
Tracking Dog 148
Tracking Dog Excellent 148
Training 61, 99
—consistency 102
—crate 94
—equipment 98
—puppy 65
Traveling 79-81
Treats 54, 98
—weaning off 106
Trichuris vulpis 130
Uncinaria stenocephala 129
United Kennel Club
—address 147
United States 12
US 16
Utility Dog 147
Utility Dog Excellent 147
Vacations 81
Vaccinations 55, 111
—sensitivity to 111
Versatile Surface Tracking title 148
Veterinarian 37, 109, 127
Von Willebrand's disease 24
Walker, Mrs. Helen Whitehouse 147
Watchdog 22
Water 72
Waters, Mrs. K.S. 19
West Highland White Terrier 10
Westminster Kennel Club dog show 144
Whining 64
Whippet 10
Whipworm **130-131**
White kennels 19
White of Sioux City 18
White's Black Midas 19
White's Black Prince 18
White, Dr. Howard S. M. 18, 19
Winners Bitch 146
Winners Class 146
Winners Dog 146
With other pets 22
With strangers 22
World War I 18
World War II 16, 18
Worm control 113

My Toy Manchester Terrier

PUT YOUR PUPPY'S FIRST PICTURE HERE

Dog's Name ______________________________

Date ______________ Photographer ______________________